CONTENTS

To those who thought they were the only ones afraid.

To anyone who's desired the courage to say yes.

*To those who were told to live life
small while yearning to live it big.*

*To anyone who wishes for fortune to favor
their bravery but needs just a little boost.*

Journey with me. You belong here.

INTRODUCTION

The time of treating fear as a private, disgraceful moral failing is over. Instead of pretending to be fearless, *Brave New You* will show you how to unlock your inner bravery with a deeper understanding about the nature of our fears and surprisingly easy-to-use tools for living with them. Our journey will help you move from awareness to knowledge and utlimately to wisdom so you can begin to navigate through today's most common fears and build a bigger, better, and more fulfilling life.

My goal is to give you the ability to dive deeper into who you are so you can courageously enjoy your life's full potential without being limited by your fears.

Brave New You is a compass for navigating the often turbulent waters of worry, unease, and panic. I, too, have been caught in the unyielding grip of self-doubt, dread, and seemingly never-ending anxious thoughts. As a biopsychologist and researcher, my solution was to jump into the science for answers, all of which I share with you here. Whether you're a seasoned captain cruising familiar fears or a newcomer to the rough seas of troubled thoughts and frightening feelings, these pages offer solace and proven strategies for charting a course through tough inner challenges. *Brave New You* speaks to the dreamer hesitant to take that first step, to the overthinker trapped in the labyrinth of what-ifs, and to anyone seeking a path to reclaim their life from the clutches of fear.

I built *Brave New You* around three simple but rarely discussed truths:

1. What we've been taught about fear is wrong.

2. Courage is not a finite resource. It is fluid and expandable.

3. Courage is a practice.

This book is divided into three sections, moving from awareness to knowledge to wisdom. In every chapter, you'll be able to dive deeper with exploration prompts in our Courage Quests while learning core neurohacks with Bravery Breaks. Neurohacks are physical and psychological non-invasive shortcuts that will boost memory, focus, and creativity and help you feel more satisfied and powerful.

Brave New You is not meant to be a textbook, but rather an opportunity to challenge your assumptions about fear, unravel every myth you've been told about it, and rebuild a braver you. This will be a narrative-driven journey, and fair warning for you hard-core science folks: I will be anthropomorphizing some anatomical and physiological processes to make them more palatable and fun for a wider audience.

Beginning with Part 1: Reimagining Fear and Courage, you'll learn how you're already hardwired for bravery. In this section, you'll build the foundations needed to dismantle the cages fear has built around you as you explore the latest research on the neurobiology and psychology of fear. Then, Part 2: The Cages of Fear will reveal the role society plays in our experience of fear and what we can do to affect positive change. Finally, in Part 3: The Keys to Courage, we accelerate our tool learning as we set out on our quest for a life where each new day becomes an opportunity to explore, learn, and grow, unburdened by the constraints of apprehension.

Our brains are not fixed—they're capable of immense change and growth. Neurohacks are like cheat codes that help you update and refresh how you think, feel, and behave in response to life's stressors.

When we break free from the cages fear has built around us, we deepen our relationships with others as authenticity replaces the need for self-protection, allowing us to foster the meaningful connections we long to build. Challenges transform from obstacles into stepping stones, leading us to uncharted territories rich with adventure and self-discovery. With courage as your compass, your journey becomes not just a passage of time but a truly great adventure.

Writing *Brave New You* was one of the hardest things I've ever done in my life because I wanted to offer you a deeper look into moments where I personally applied the tools you find in this book. Never before have I put words to many of the tender experiences you'll read here. I felt it essential to be vulnerable, openhearted, and brave since I'm asking the same of you. I was raised to hide my true self, to only show a polished, shiny version of me to everyone—all the time. But I now know that is not how one flourishes. We humans love stories, and we thrive when we feel connected. So this book is part how-to, part story, and entirely about making you feel less alone in your struggles to navigate life's every day worries. Come with me as I run from a bear, jump out of a plane, examine how my own fears held me back, and, hardest of all, navigate a complicated maternal relationship from start to finish.

Brave New You is also a kind of culmination of my own fear practice, written for the person I once was, who was forever trying to navigate unfamiliar spaces without a map. My goal is to guide you to a future that is brigher and bolder than you ever thought possible. This book gives you permission to embrace your fear as a normal human emotion, while providing you with the tools to minimize the time you spend in discomfort. In fact, you're going to feel your fear with wild abandon, knowing you will be stronger on the other side of it.

For me, mastering my ordinary fears was the key to unlocking success and happiness beyond my wildest dreams, both in my career and my personal life. I soon realized that the tools and strategies I developed could help others transform how they respond to new opportunities, risk-taking, and change. Through my work, I've empowered tens of thousands to embrace their fear and take action to transform their life using the very tools you will find in this book.

No one has all the answers, including me. But what I do know is that the way we speak, think, and live with fear requires sweeping change. This begins by ceasing to pretend that fear doesn't exist. For too long we've been made to believe that fear is a dark, intangible force that, by its very nature, is too difficult to handle. Even worse, we're taught that feeling fear is shameful and should be endured in silence. Instead, let us radically reimagine fear in a way that allows us to leverage our bodies' natural responses for better health, confidence, and resilience.

Brave New You was created to give you the tools you need to become the architect of your own desitny. So, it's time to let go of everything you thought you knew about fear and come with me as we create a more courageous tomorrow.

Honestly, could anything be braver?

PART ONE

Reimagining Fear and Courage

CHAPTER 1

Fear Is Your Ally

To soar toward what's possible, you must
leave behind what's comfortable.
—CICELY TYSON

Regardless of whether it's mental or physical, fear is often cast as the ominous adversary, a formidable force threatening to freeze us in place or make us run away screaming. However, within the shadowy realms of trepidation lies a profound paradox—fear, when harnessed and understood, can emerge as an unexpected ally on the journey of self-discovery and growth.

Fear is one of the most primal and powerful emotions humans experience. It alerts us to danger and motivates us to take action—two critical facets for survival dating back to our species' earliest days. However, much of what is socially taught about fear ranges from completely wrong to wildly unhelpful. As kids, we're taught that fear is an undesirable, even shameful, emotion. So, we grow into adults who see fear as a sign of weakness, something to be avoided, escaped, or conquered—but never discussed and always hidden. We go through life feeling like we're the only ones to be scared of the unknown or terrified we're not good enough. But I have a secret for you; neither of us are alone. In fact, *we're all afraid of being afraid.*

Just as a compass guides explorers through uncharted territories, fear can serve as a tool, pointing toward what you need to transform your life. This nuanced perspective invites you to reconsider fear not as a hindrance but as a potential ally, capable of awakening dormant strengths and propelling you toward unforeseen triumphs. Embarking on a voyage of self-discovery, you may find fear—when embraced and transformed—becomes a steadfast companion on the path to the life you dream of.

I know I did.

My Story

I was raised in a house ruled by fear. Researching it became a way to dissolve its hold on me.

Although I wouldn't know this story until my eighteenth birthday, I was adopted at birth by my maternal grandmother, whom I call Momma Helen, and her husband, Les. At 16 years old, my birth mother was a child herself and already struggling to raise her first son. So, when Momma Helen and Les lost their toddler son to a swimming accident, adopting me seemed like a perfect balm to their grief.

However, just three months after I was adopted, Les also died. I can't tell you what Momma Helen was like before losing her son and husband in the span of just two short years, but I can tell you how I was raised: to be afraid of everything.

Afraid to be authentic or vulnerable. Afraid of being human.

Momma Helen's fearfulness manifested in many troubling ways, but one of the most damaging was raising me with the idea that the world is *always* a scary place, and that to show any emotion other than happiness was a weakness.

As an adult, I used facts and irrefutable logic as a means of creating a defense against vulnerability. As a result, in my protective bubble of rational clarity, I also became really, really bad at understanding my own emotions—which was probably why I found science so appealing! Science as a discipline demands and rewards removing oneself and one's emotions from the work. This was wonderful for me . . . at first.

I began my professional career at NASA as part of the payload research team for the Space Shuttle *Columbia* Mission STS-107 before taking a biology faculty position at San Jose State University just before my twenty-seventh birthday. However, I discovered my personal achievements didn't make me feel any more whole as a person.

If emotions were colors, it was like I had been seeing only two shades of the rainbow my whole life. And though I kept telling myself those two colors were enough, inside I knew it wasn't true. I wanted more. So, like any good scientist, I began to study emotions to learn how to understand, feel, and express them across the entire spectrum.

Here is what I learned.

The Normal Fears of Life

In this book, there is no fear too great or too small.

All fears are valid, but we don't have to be at their mercy. Here's the secret to mastering any fear: Instead of ignoring it—embrace it, question it, and work to understand it. Is it rational or irrational? Where is this fear coming from? As we dive deeper into these questions, we find that there are three main sources of fear: biological, cultural, and personal.

TIER 1: BIOLOGICAL FEAR

Fear, a primal and adaptive emotion, is rooted in the complex landscape of our biology. Evolution has finely tuned our brains to ensure survival by triggering the fear-arousal response when confronted with danger, whether it's real or simply *perceived* as real. This system also helps us learn by committing threatening experiences to memory for future recall and risk avoidance.

As we move through the world, this biological machinery—which we'll learn more about in the pages to come—allows us to recognize, react, and learn from fear-inducing situations. Unfortunately, our human machine runs on ancient software and can overreact to the triggers of modern life. The human brain evolved to notice and respond to unfamiliar sounds to ensure survival, especially loud or sudden ones. But now, it must work harder to process the near constant booms from TV shows we're not watching, the blares from someone else's music, or the beeps of an after-hours email alert. The human brain also helps to ensure survival by being able to respond to fast-moving objects, but what's a brain to do when everything from scooters to cars to trains are constantly speeding by during an average day?

Here's the secret to mastering any fear: Instead of ignoring it—embrace it, question it, and work to understand it.

Your brain simply wants to keep you safe and alive. And though we can rationalize that the sudden ping of your phone alert left on high volume in the middle of the night won't harm you, your fear-arousal system doesn't know that. Recognizing that fear is simply an aspect of a normal, functioning human body helps us to let go of any shame or moral responsibility we might be carrying around about feeling afraid, worried, or anxious.

TIER 2: CULTURAL FEAR

We live in a world where we're increasingly socialized to sanitize, downplay, and ignore our feelings of distress and dismay. At the same time, external forces like media and consumer culture relentlessly play on our insecurities, to win the most clicks and sell the most products.

From childhood until we shuffle off this mortal coil, we learn what is "safe" and "dangerous" through social cues and stories from those around us—our parents, teachers, and friends, as well as from books, television, and movies.

The idea that something should be feared—fictional or not—can be presented in every form of communication we have. As time goes on, these cues are increasingly ingrained in us until they become automatic responses. Redefining the stories we've internalized as truths and filtering out future fear-driven messages are essential steps for developing a more courageous mind.

TIER 3: PERSONAL FEAR

Personal fears are unique to us and dependent on our individual experiences, personalities, and outlook. For example, I might fear upsetting people while you could feel right at home rocking every boat you board.

The most insidious personal fears are not the large, life-threatening ones that we associate with external physical survival (like running from a bear) but the smaller, everyday fears that creep into the most mundane aspects of our lives, limiting our potential. These internal personal fears are where *Brave New You* can help the most—with fears we feel but don't really talk about or admit.

A few examples of personal fears that commonly shape our thoughts, behaviors, and actions are:

- **Failure:** The fear of not meeting expectations, personal or professional, can easily lead to anxiety and self-doubt. Giving in to this fear sacrifices our opportunity to learn from our mistakes and grow stronger for it.

- **Success:** Paradoxically, the fear of success can be as overwhelming as the fear of failure, as one worries about the new expectations and responsibilities that come with achieving their goals.

- **Change:** It's easy to fear the unknown and the disruptions that come with major life changes, whether it's a career shift, relocation, or reshaping a relationship. Fearing change can keep us trapped in our comfort zones, hindering our progress and growth.

- **Rejection:** Rooted in a fear of being unlovable or worthless, those who refuse to navigate through this fear shy away from taking strategic risks that result in positive outcomes.

- **Loneliness:** The fear of being isolated or alone can influence decisions related to social activities, relationships, and even career choices.

- **Uncertainty:** Ambiguity and unpredictability can trigger anxiety in those who crave stability and a sense of control over their lives.

- **Judgment or Criticism:** The fear of being negatively evaluated by others can inhibit personal expression and authentic self-representation.

- **Abandonment:** Rooted in attachment patterns, the fear of being abandoned or left behind can impact relationships and emotional well-being.

"NEUROHACK" YOUR WAY TO NEW HABITS AND BEHAVIORS

What if you could get to feeling braver, faster?

Throughout *Brave New You*, I will share my favorite "neurohacks"—physical and psychological shortcuts that will boost memory, focus, and creativity, and help you feel more satisfied and powerful. These neurohacks optimize your body's natural processes for peak performance and improved mental health through science and technology.

Our brains are not fixed—they're capable of change and growth. Neurohacks are like cheat codes that help you update and refresh how you think, feel, and behave in response to life's stresses.

So, what does this look like in daily life? In my case, they helped me overcome uncomfortable things that I would simply not do before neurohacking. Things like asking for my worth or sharing my needs and desires with others.

The neurohacks I'll share throughout this book were strategically chosen and developed to help reduce stress levels, increase creativity and motivation, and even help you learn new things more quickly and effectively. And because neurohacking is a non-invasive method to fine-tune your brain, there are no major risks in trying it.

But they are not a panacea. My neurohacks, while powerful, are not meant to diagnose or treat clinical fear, such as entrenched phobias or clinical anxiety. I am not a clinical psychologist who treats patients. What I am is an expert in navigating everyday fear by using the very latest science applied to those moments when we wish we could be a little braver, bolder, and more present—in short, to have a more courageous mind.

We will never be able to turn off our primal fear reaction (and wouldn't want to), but we *can* change the way we respond to fear. We can learn to manage it, make peace with it, and even use it to our advantage. One of the many things I love about neurohacking is the experimentation.

Not everything will work for everybody. But we don't get to the "aha" moments or the "that changed my life" breakthroughs without experimenting. Trying, failing, and trying again is how we transform and transcend.

As I tell my university students, the process is the point.

Fact and Fiction: The Two Sides of Fear

We all experience fear, but the fear we experience is not always the same. In fact, there are two distinct categories of fear: factual fear and fictional fear. And being able to tell the two apart is crucial.

Answer these deeper-dive questions based on who you are right now:

1. Are you confident in your ability to recognize and navigate your challenging emotions?

2. How do you currently manage your fear?

3. Do you effectively express your emotions to the people in your life? If so, how?

4. Which emotions do you find most challenging to feel and/or express?

5. Do you find yourself frequently overwhelmed by those challenging emotions?

6. What are your coping mechanisms for reducing your everyday stress?

The simple act of forcing our brains to decide between the two choices can actually kick us out of a fear spiral. Sure, there are plenty of reasons to be afraid. But sometimes our minds activate a fear response without a real need for it, leading to poor decision making, escalation, and yet more fear.

Here's the difference between factual fear and fictional fear:

Factual fear: Factual fear keeps us safe from harm that is happening in the moment and in a shared reality with others, not just in our own thoughts. Examples of factual fear would be the terror you might feel if you had to run across an eight-lane freeway during rush hour. Or the dread that washes over you when you run a red light and instantly see a traffic officer pull behind you. Even if you've never done either of these, the fear of negative repercussions keeps you from doing them. If you're walking through a dark alley at night and hear footsteps, your natural reaction is to feel afraid. That's factual fear telling you that you could be in danger and to be careful. Factual fear is beneficial because it helps us avoid threatening or dangerous situations. Without it, we would regularly put ourselves in harm's way.

Fictional fear: Fictional fears are those fears we have that are not rooted in a shared reality. Although they may have been inspired by a factual event or story, fictional fears tend to exist only in our minds and are not part of the here and now that we share with others.

One way fictional fear shows up in our daily lives is when we ruminate. "Ruminating," what many refer to as worry, is a term that describes being stuck in a loop of obsessive thoughts about causes, consequences, and possible solutions for an extended period of time. When we're stuck in a rumination loop, we can't help but dwell on past experiences or unresolved issues as we struggle to gain insight or predict possible future outcomes. Rumination is a self-defeating pattern that can lead to heightened levels of stress, depression, and anxiety. It's a state of thinking where your mind can easily slide down the worst-case-scenario rabbit hole, activating your body's physical fear response and leaving you feeling tense and depleted.

Look, we've all been there—lying in bed ruminating over a comment made by a friend, trying to decode what they really meant or second-guessing something we said in a work meeting. We replay the scene over and over again in our mind, which results in feeling even more anxious and dreading future interactions.

If you're prone to rumination, like me, it's important to arm yourself with strategies that can help you redirect your attention away from ruminating thoughts and create space for healthier thinking patterns, like the "neurohacks" we'll present throughout this book. Once you add these techniques to your toolbox, along with self-care basics like deep breathing, meditation, journaling, and exercise, you'll find yourself better able to connect with friends, colleagues, and loved ones, and to engage in all the things that bring you joy.

Fictional fear is what we experience when we're afraid of going after our dreams or when we're too afraid to take risks.

Fictional fear as a category is often based on false assumptions or past experiences that no longer apply to our current situation. In the extreme, they can also venture into the irrational. For example, a common fictional fear is being deathly afraid of speaking up in a meeting as an adult because you were ostracized for speaking up in your third-grade class. Other examples of fictional fears are those around success (or "imposter syndrome")—the fear of failure, of change, or of rejection. Fictional fear is what we experience when we're afraid of going after our dreams or when we're too afraid to take risks.

FACT VS. FICTION: A BEAR IN THE WOODS

My partner, Craig, decided to mark the passing of his most recent trip around the sun by climbing California's Mount Whitney, the tallest peak in the 48 contiguous states, up and down in one day. This was not my kind of hike, but being the supportive partner that I am, I dropped off Craig and his son Riely at the trailhead five hours before dawn and watched their shadowy figures disappear up the trail on their quest to reach the summit by lunchtime.

Although cell service was nearly nonexistent at higher elevations, the sporadic texts I got assured me that they were on target for a dinnertime arrival back at base camp. Their hike totaled twenty-two miles in a single day, so I wanted to solidify my status as all-time best base camp girlfriend by having a deliciously hot meal waiting for them when they arrived. To this end, I drove into the tiny nearby town of Lone Pine to purchase a meat lover's pizza for Craig and his son as a triumphant birthday surprise.

I sped back up the mountain, pizza in tow, just as the summer sun was setting over the craggy peaks of Mount Whitney. I recall the warm scent of California sage mingled with the life-giving aromas of pepperoni, sausage, bacon, and mozzarella as I made my way into the base camp parking lot. I was so caught up in my daydream that I didn't notice a man chattering away at me as he walked over. He had a gray beard longer than my arm and an omnipresent air reminiscent of Gandalf the Grey, California-style.

Since I hadn't been listening the first time, I responded with the classic, "I'm sorry, what?"

"Do you have food in there?" he asked, gesturing toward my car.

"Oh, uh, yeah," I said. "I have a pizza."

"I wouldn't leave it in there," he advised, with a gray eyebrow raised. "Go put it in the bear box—it's just over there."

Bristling, I thought but didn't say, "Thanks, bro. I'm a biologist, I know how to nature." Instead, I politely declined, explaining that I wouldn't be there long, that I was just waiting for some hikers to arrive.

"That's a really bad idea," Mount Whitney Gandalf replied. "A bear could tear open that BMW like opening a can of soup."

Smiling begrudgingly, I replied, "Sure, guess it couldn't hurt," before sauntering over to the bear box, plopping the extra-large pizza box inside, and shutting the massive metal door with a large clang.

Then I lay in a nearby wildflower meadow and watched the sun dip below the horizon, while keeping an eye on the trailhead, waiting for the boys to return. And return they did, minutes before the sky went fully dark. I left them by the car while I went to retrieve the pizza. Practically skipping to the bear box, I imagined all the praise and adoration that was about to come my way.

Made of thick, gray steel, the bear box stood about four feet tall and stretched back around five feet wide. Because it was high summer, a popular time for visitors, the box was stuffed. My pizza box had been pushed to the very back, forcing me to crawl inside to grab it. Stretching my body up to the waist inside, my fingertips nearly there, I heard urgent, loud yelling behind me. As it was not in a language I could understand, I didn't really think anything of it. Finally grabbing the box, I wiggled out and looked up to see a full-grown black bear perched on the box, inches from my face.

This is when my factual fear response kicked in.

Pulling the pizza free from the bear box, I slammed the metal door so hard the clang reverberated through my ears as I sprinted back to the car at top speed, yelling, "BEAR! START THE CAR!! BEEAARRRRRRR!!!" Craig and Riely both jumped into the car—no questions asked—as I barrel-rolled into the backseat with the pizza. Craig hit the accelerator and in a voice calmer than it should have been, inquired, "Did you just steal a pizza from a bear?"

Indignant, I panted, "No! It's my pizza, and no way was that bear getting this $45 pizza!"

In the fraction of a second it took for me to grab that meat-za and run, my brain completed a feat of chemical and hormonal acrobatics designed to prime my body for survival. I felt threatened, and my brain unleashed its fight-or-flight response, flooding my system with adrenaline and cortisol that powered me to the car unharmed. This sounds impressive, but I merely did what evolution primed me to do.

Factual fears—like being chased by a bear—exist in our shared reality and happen in real time, not in our past or future. Our bodies know exactly what to do when factual fear strikes. Factual fears are also easier to talk about and accept because they're considered more "legitimate" by polite society. When a genuinely life-threatening event occurs, everyone agrees that you should be afraid without question or shame.

HOW TO TELL THE DIFFERENCE

Both fictional and factual fears have the potential to keep us safe, but they can also keep us trapped in cages of our own making. Yes, there are plenty of things worth being afraid of—the key is learning how to let our fictional fears act like a strong wind that moves us forward instead of quicksand that keeps us stuck. And though fictional fears may be rooted in truth on some level, they keep us from getting where we want to go, from becoming who we want to be. Thankfully, fictional fears are also the ones that we have the most power to change.

But how can you tell the difference between a factual fear and a fictional fear? A good rule of thumb: Focusing on a factual fear disappears once the danger has passed and you return to safety. For example, I didn't spend the rest of the night ruminating on whether or not the Mount Whitney bear was angry with me for running away because this was a factual, in-the-moment fear. Another example would be if you had to quickly slam on your brakes to avoid trading bumper paint with another driver. You'd feel afraid during the experience. But afterward you'd return to your day and not give it another thought—because it's a factual fear. However, if

Bravery Break: Pinching the Valley (HeGu Meridian)

The HeGu Meridian, also known as "the Valley," is located between the thumb and index finger on both hands. The benefits of massaging this pressure point are supported by both traditional Chinese medicine and science. Specifically, massaging the HeGu Meridian helps stimulate the vagus nerve, your body's longest cranial nerve, via the radial nerve in your hands. Massaging the HeGu Meridian can signal the production of feel-good neurotransmitters, disengage your brain's default mode network (DMN), and activate your parasympathetic nervous system (the aspect of your nervous system responsible for your sense of calm, rest, and digestion, which is opposite of the fight-or-flight response). We'll go more in depth on all this later (see page 168), but I want you to have a quick-win neurohack now. I personally use this technique a lot, especially if I happen to wake up at 3:00 a.m. and my mind is racing about all the things I haven't done or that embarrassing thing I said a year ago that no one remembers but me.

To get all the courage-building, fear-reducing benefits of a HeGu Meridian massage, first find the pressure point by placing your thumb on the back of your hand and your index finger on the palm side at the lowest point of the valley created by your thumb and forefinger (i.e., your index finger). The magic spot is below the webbing toward the base of your thumb. Apply firm pressure and massage in a circular motion for thirty to sixty seconds. Then repeat on the other hand. Go ahead and try it now, and see if you notice a difference in your stress levels!

you can't shake the fear of being "not good enough" at work after you were talked over at a meeting, leaving you to agonize constantly about losing your job, you're experiencing a fictional fear that will continue to hold you back.

With fictional fears, thoughts and emotions linger long after the perceived threat is gone. Learning to distinguish between factual and fictional fear is an important skill, because fictional fears can have very negative effects in our lives. Fictional fears can be even more insidious to our mental health and happiness than factual fears. However, once we learn to identify the source of our fictional fears, we can work on addressing them head-on.

Ready to Break Your Fear Cycle?

Embracing fear as an ally is the transformative key to unlocking your fullest potential.

By acknowledging its presence and understanding its messages, you can harness fear's energy to propel you toward growth and success instead of wasting that energy on worrying or hiding from opportunities.

Fear isn't a roadblock— it's a stepping stone to an extraordinary life.

You're already strong enough to confront the unknown and emerge bolder, wiser, and more resilient. You've done it before, and you absolutely can do it again.

In the next chapter, you will explore the art of recognizing, examining, and reframing the stories that no longer serve your courageous life. These stories may be from your past, from your circle of loved ones, the media you enjoy, or stories you continue to tell yourself on near constant repeat, ultimately influencing your actions and keeping you trapped in a fear cycle. We can only escape this fear cycle through new thoughts, new words, and, yes, new actions. Since change can be difficult, I will make this process way easier with the actionable steps found in our Courage Quests and neurohack heavy Bravery Breaks.

I'm incredibly excited to be your guide on this journey because when we heal ourselves, we can't help but heal those around us.

Fear isn't a roadblock—it's a stepping stone to an extraordinary life.

Ready to put your best foot forward?

CHAPTER 2

Fearless Is a Facade

Some of us are not living our dreams
because we're living our fears.
—LES BROWN

I was once asked if courage was the opposite of fear. After a brief pause, I responded with a resounding "no." It's easy to think of courage and fear as opposites, but in truth they're more intertwined, like two stalks of a growing vine.

Courage comes from facing and moving through the tough parts of life. It's neither finite nor static. You are not simply born with it or without it, since it's fluid and can be strengthened throughout your life with practice and tools.

Too often in Western culture, fear is seen as a negative and irrational emotion to be avoided at all costs, or something that causes people to repress their authentic experiences instead of talking openly about them. We even shy away from saying the word "fear" and instead substitute a catchall term such as "stress" or a euphemism like "freaking out." But feeling afraid is not shameful. It is an evolutionary response meant to protect us from danger. It's not our fault we were raised in a world that barely acknowledges this very human trait, let alone encourages open discussion and exploration of it.

Our fear-repression culture has been further exacerbated by technological advancements, leading many people to feel pressure to present a brave face to the world. From managing stress to navigating difficult relationships, being able to understand and respond courageously can help us take control of our lives and live more moments with vitality.

When we reexamine the way we interact with fear and then start managing our relationship with it, we can begin to unlock the fear "cages" created by our biology, society, families, and ourselves. We need to stop equating fear with weakness or incompetence and start seeing it for what it really is: an opportunity for growth, resilience, and transformation.

To know courage, we must know fear.

When I was asked the earlier question about courage being the opposite of fear, I wish I had responded that the opposite of fear is exhilaration—the feeling of immense freedom, excitement, and expansive joy. We sacrifice the ecstasy of playing in the ocean surf for the illusion of safety in the rock cave. We abandon our chance to laugh until our eyes fill with tears for the false security of disconnection and hiding who we truly are.

Living in cages built of fear keeps us from the vitality of life that is our birthright. Fortunately, you can start the demolition of these cages. Grab a hammer and let's get swinging.

The Myth of Fearlessness

We are inundated with messages that tell us to be fearless. From ads to coffee mugs to T-shirts, we're urged to have no fear in our careers, in our relationships, throughout our entire lives. The assumption here is that being fearless is the ultimate goal, that a lack of fear ensures success. I used to think this way. I believed that if I could just ignore and hide my fear, and create the illusion of fearlessness, I'd be fine. Clearly, everyone around me had their fear thing figured out without any help. So, I thought, if I just keep pretending I'm fearless around others, then surely one day I would achieve this blissful state.

But what if being fearless isn't actually possible? What if fearless is just a facade?

In late 2022, the sportswear brand PUMA launched its Generation Fearless campaign with the tagline "Find Your Fearless." The adrenaline-laced ad encouraged viewers to "be fearless" in the face of challenges while showcasing professional soccer stars like Sara Björk and Neymar. As a massive Super Bowl–style gold ring spun across the screen engraved with the words "Fearless World Champion," the music crescendoed and viewers were bombarded with quick-cut images of young people having the time of their lives. A dramatic voice ended the ad with "You have to be fearless if you want great things to happen."

> **But what if being fearless isn't actually possible? What if fearless is just a facade?**

The myth at the heart of this ad: Only those who are fearless can be successful and whole. Conversely, if you are afraid then you're broken. What the commercial didn't show were the years of training and hard work required to become a professional athlete. It didn't mention the countless hours Björk and Neymar spent honing their skills, or the bruises and setbacks they endured along the way. Instead, the commercial perpetuated a pernicious myth: that being fearless unlocks human potential, and some people are born courageous while others are not. Which simply isn't true.

Courage is not an inherent trait—it's something that can be learned and developed over time.

When I began my fear journey, I was far from fearless. I didn't feel remotely brave, so I figured I'd fake it until I made it. I thought that dangerous stunts like jumping out of a plane would prove that I was fearless and thus make me so. But it didn't work out that way. In fact, this pursuit of vanquishing my fears was fruitless and downright exhausting. Eventually, I realized that this approach was costing me more than it was worth in time, mental health, and even my professional and personal success. Because behind my tough, inauthentic exterior was a lot of fear and insecurity. It was until I finally learned to embrace my fear—by knowing and accepting that fearlessness doesn't exist—that I came to see fear as an empowering force and not a debilitating one.

Courage is not an inherent trait—it's something that can be learned and developed over time.

When you examine "the myth of fearlessness" through the lens of neurobiology, it completely breaks down because sustained fearlessness is close to biologically impossible. It simply doesn't exist, save in an extremely rare genetic disorder called Urbach-Wiethe disease, which leaves those stricken with the inability to feel fear. It's so rare that only 400 cases have been reported since it was first discovered in 1929.

In the absence of a medical condition, the closest we can get to true fearlessness is when we're eating, a benign process that signals to our brains that we're safe enough to momentarily consume fuel. However, as soon as we swallow a single bite, our incredibly fleeting moment of fearlessness vanishes, leaving us in the same emotional state we were in before we began. In practice, the myth of fearlessness sets up not just an unrealistic expectation, but a biologically impossible one.

But perhaps the worst part of the fearlessness myth is how we beat ourselves up when we can't be fearless. Despite our best efforts at "choosing to be fearless," fear inevitably creeps into our lives, leaving us feeling like we've failed and inviting shame to snuggle up next to our daily anxiety and stress. This often leads to us doubling down and repressing our feelings of fear even further.

WHEN THE CHUTE DOESN'T OPEN

I had just arrived at SkyDive Chicago after a late-night drive from O'Hare. I was meeting a group of friends for my first skydiving experience the next morning. I hadn't been there long when I found myself staring dumbfounded at my friend Will, who was describing his day and also why the whole camp was in celebration mode.

"Wait, I'm sorry, did you just say you almost died today?" I asked.

He responded with the calm of someone who's come across the divide: "Yes. I mean, I was scared out of my mind when my main parachute wouldn't deploy! That was the first time I had to use my reserve on a jump, and I would prefer never to have my main malfunction at 10,000 feet again!"

Then someone I didn't know came up to Will and high-fived him while shouting, "My fearless bro!" The line was delivered with reverence and respect, as if fearlessness was a holy altar at which only a few can worship. That to be fearless meant you did a hard thing but felt no angst, trepidation, or anxiety.

That night, I crawled into my tent alongside the other skydivers, pondering what Will had gone through that day and his attitude about it. He never once claimed to be fearless; in fact, he was very open and honest about the pure terror he felt. He did not feel the need to hide his true experience behind a facade of feigned fearlessness. Of course, it can be easier to be honest about your fear with something as easily understood as nearly plummeting into the earth with nothing to save you. It is a wee bit harder to be publicly open about internal fears, like not being good enough or being unlovable.

Six in the morning came much too quickly, and it was time to suit up and jump. After a brief training session on how to operate my tandem parachute (they don't let newbies jump solo, of course), we boarded a tiny seatless plane, where I was sandwiched between two men I had just met. As the plane climbed higher, my bravery sank. Soon it was my turn, and I approached the bay door, peering down at the distant land below. My heart raced and my stomach churned. I wanted to turn back, but it was go time. I stood on the edge of the open plane door bursting with a mix of excitement, terror, and anticipation. My instructor said we'd jump on the count of five (though I'm pretty sure he only counted to three before flinging us both into the abyss).

Before I could fully process what was happening, we were freefalling. As the wind whipped through my hair and clothes, nothing else mattered to my brain except staying alive. But then my terror slowly changed into awe as the world seemed to be stretching out forever beneath us. Once I stopped screaming, I felt oddly and completely at peace and connected to something much larger than myself. After a period of time that was paradoxically too short and too long, I was given the thumbs up that it was time to deploy the chutes, and we gently drifted down to the landing zone.

Back on solid ground, I felt a sense of pride that I'd gone through with the jump in spite of my trepidation. And a realization that my exhilarating experience wasn't made possible because I was fearless. It happened because I had chosen to be courageous despite my fear. In that moment, I recognized for certain that fearlessness does not exist. I also realized that I'd just sprained my ankle in the soft grass, reminding me that the best life lessons come with a cost.

We're All Afraid of Being Afraid

When was the last time you said the "F-word" out loud? No, not that one. The other one, the scarier one.

Our conversations about fear (*that* "F-word") are dysfunctional. Or nonexistent. Too often, we don't feel confident talking about the "F-word" because there's so much shame associated with fear in our Western society. We've never been taught how to deal with alarm and dread in a healthy way. So our fear is underreported, and too many of us are out of touch with our feelings of fear. Typically, we can't even talk about fear without making others uncomfortable. The word itself is intolerable.

Here's a quick test: Do you ever feel as if the only time it's culturally appropriate to be afraid is when watching a horror movie or riding a roller coaster?

These kinds of fear-inducing events are cathartic because the feeling you might experience while watching *Scream* or riding The Death Plunge is ultimately under your control. If you get too scared, you can always leave the theater or ask to get off the ride.

As much as we'd like to put all our fearful emotions into a box that we only open when we want to, life doesn't work that way. Fear is like the prank where an inflatable snake pops out from a tube of chips. Your fear doesn't care what you were expecting or how much control you thought you had.

The unexpectedness of fear is exacerbated by the fact that we're constantly inundated with societal messages that trigger our fears, particularly when they tell us that we need to be perfect—the perfect body, the perfect job, the perfect life.

Add in how we're socialized to equate fear with weakness, to see it as an unwelcome emotion at best and a sign of moral failure at worst, and it's no wonder that we feel pressure to deny fear in order to appear flawless. I refer to this toxic mix as the "social sanitization of fear" (social sanitization is the process of making oneself acceptable to one's social group). In the age of social media, with our networks expanding to global proportions, we can sometimes feel the need to present a brave face to the *entire* world.

The way we talk about fear is also dysfunctional. We've all been there: You feel overwhelmed by a big project, unsure if you have the time, talent, or resources to finish it. You meet your best friend for a quick coffee, a small luxury as your deadline looms, and as soon as you sit down they blurt out, "Wow, you look really stressed!"

If you're like me, you immediately launch into word vomit mode to share all your pent-up feelings of overwhelming dread. But why do we use the word "stress" instead of "fear"? One explanation is that "stress" has become a more socially acceptable term than "fear," along with associated adjectives like "dread" and "anxiousness." Stress isn't an emotion, after all—it's a physiological response to external stimuli. However, most of us are more comfortable using the word "stress" because it implies that we can manage or cope with the situation without much support.

Language has the power to shape our understanding of the world around us—including our emotions. For many people, "fear" connotes a negative, irrational emotion that should be avoided or downplayed. And yet we continue to use the word "stress" as a euphemism for "fear." "Stress" is less emotionally charged, so it helps us maintain a sense of control over how we perceive ourselves. By using the word "stress" instead of "fear," we present our emotional experience in a more positive light for ourselves and those around us. This also leaves our conversations around fear steeped in dysfunction, one that is rarely mentioned out loud or even acknowledged.

Stress isn't an emotion, after all— it's a physiological response to external stimuli.

For me, dinnertime conversations growing up were never a forum for discussing my struggles with angst or anxiety, and there were certainly no stress management seminars offered to me in college. When admitting fearful emotions is seen as a weakness, our shared language becomes euphemistic. Maybe we believe that if we hide our fear behind words like "stressed," the words will make the fear less scary. But doing so just prolongs our suffering and rarely improves our lives.

So we sanitize our fear by taking it in small acceptable doses, such as watching a scary movie with friends or going to a haunted house for Halloween. Sanitizing our everyday fears, which allows us to ignore them, is such an ingrained norm in Western society that most of us do it without realizing it. Instead of acknowledging the scary, sometimes terrifying aspects of modern living, we're basically expected to pretend that we aren't afraid of anything.

Worse, when we focus too much on social sanitization, we miss important opportunities for growth. Why? Because social sanitization limits creativity and expression, discourages risk-taking, promotes conformity instead of individuality, and ultimately leads to even greater feelings of anxiety and insecurity.

We admire and reward bravery, idolizing heroes and heroines who don't back down in the face of tremendous opposition, who put their own safety aside and do what needs to be done to save the kingdom/city/world. We tend to see these people as born brave, with extra-special powers somehow ordained by the universe. We're led to believe that these exceptional people never feel fear, and that those of us cursed with feelings of fear must endure a lifetime of being weak and powerless. That is wrong on multiple levels. No one is "born brave," and fear is not a moral failing; it reflects how our brains have evolved to survive and thrive.

> *No one is "born brave," and fear is not a moral failing; it reflects how our brains have evolved to survive and thrive.*

As we journey together to learn, unlearn, and redefine everything we know about fear and courage, I want you to keep three extremely important points in mind:

1: FEAR IS HOW WE SURVIVE

Each of us is neurobiologically wired to feel fear, which means that experiencing fear is healthy! Fear helps us make decisions that keep us safe and protect us from harm. Fear helps us decide to toss out that chicken salad sandwich from last week because we don't want to risk food poisoning. Fear reminds us to put on safety belts and encourages us to save for retirement. The idea that certain special people in the world are naturally courageous or fearless is just plain false. Contrary to popular belief, fear is the best defense mechanism we have!

When we start to perceive the sensation of fear as being like any other bodily function, we begin to unlearn the shame we've been taught to associate with it—a powerful first step.

2: COURAGE IS FLUID

I have three favorite ecosystems: tropical, marine, and the crisp, fresh-flowing rivers we biology nerds call riparian (I'm basically a water nymph). One of my favorite hikes is to trundle along a river's lush riparian zone. Unlike those trails that cut through open fields or crest rolling hills, a riparian trail is usually very crooked, unpredictable, and boggy from start to finish as the river expands and contracts. Our courage is much like a riparian trail with its swelling and receding river waters, in the sense that some seasons of our life, or even parts of the same day, find us with bravery in abundance while others find our courage reduced to a trickle.

Courage is neither finite nor fixed, and it is not innate. This fluidity means that courage can change—and be learned. Yes, you can have natural tendencies toward bravery in some aspects of life, but everyone can learn to be even braver. Just like hiking uneven, gnarly riparian zones will build glorious glutes faster than couch surfing, building your courage muscles through practices that challenge and engage you will be even more accelerated with the right tools and knowledge.

3: THE ROOTS OF ALL OUR HUMAN FEARS

When we dig deeper into our most common everyday fears, we see two distinct emotional experiences at the root of our fears: the fear of losing control and the fear of not being enough. Sometimes it's a messy combination of both. I know it doesn't feel that way when fear is hijacking your brain, but it really is that simple. However, when we learn to pause and decide which bucket our current fear falls into, it de-escalates, allowing our brain to downshift into a state of courage.

TRUE CRIME AND MURDER MYSTERIES MAKE US FEEL SAFE

Cozy murder mysteries are one of my favorite genres of audiobook (I say audiobook because I love being able to *read* while walking my dog, Bandit, or cleaning, because let's face it, cleaning is my cardio!).

I only consume the "cozy" kind because they don't go into the actual details of violence and there's usually a plucky female protagonist who's never solved a case before but gets the culprit in the end, which makes me feel like, "Hey, that could totally be me!" Like me, countless otherwise well-adjusted, non-murderous, productive members of society regularly snuggle up on their couches to watch, listen to, and read stories of true crime and the fiction they inspire. But why are we so fascinated by these dark stories? Why are we drawn to the most depraved act one human can inflict upon another? Can we use this to our advantage to feel more courageous?

As it turns out, there are documented benefits of consuming true crime and murder mysteries beyond simple entertainment.

These stories help us make sense of tragedy

Part of the appeal of dark content is the human desire to make sense of tragedy, particularly when that tragedy seems profound yet avoidable. Take, for an all-too-common example, an active shooter incident. It seems paradoxical, but we feel safer by getting a little closer to senseless acts of violence, in part because they help us understand the psychology of those who carry out the acts. That closeness allows us to regain a sense of control over acts of violence by exploring and sometimes understanding why they happen. Just like zombie films help us practice how we would escape a horde, true crime brings a sense of calm and control because we feel like we're taking action to be more prepared, which makes us feel safer.

It doesn't always feel this way, but the United States and the world as a whole has gotten consistently safer over time. According to the FBI's annual crime statistics, the rate of violent crime in the United States dropped from 758 offenses per 100,000 people in 1991 to 398 offenses per 100,000 people in 2020. That's a 47 percent decrease. Of course this doesn't mean that crime is gone altogether or that true crime media isn't booming in print, audio, and on the screen. At times, it can feel like bootcamp for future frightening possibilities. Women often feel most vulnerable to violent crimes, which may explain why many female readers, listeners, and viewers are

Bravery Break: One Step at a Time

In the 2018 documentary *Notorious RBG*, Ruth Bader Ginsburg said, "Real change, enduring change, happens one step at a time." This is true of all types of change, including the change that is required to strengthen your courageous mind.

As you strive to become braver, identify an activity that slightly scares you, something just beyond your comfort zone but not truly terrifying. Visualize this activity and the fear it brings. This exercise aims to gradually train your brain to fear it less, helping you build courage progressively.

This comfort zone–pushing activity will vary from one person to the next. For me, anything that breaks with the social norms of being a "good girl" is mildly scary (no surprise, given my upbringing). When I engage in this courage-building practice, I try to do things that break with that "good girl" stereotype. Instead of saying "yes" to everyone around me and ignoring my own needs, I practice saying "no." I say no to the fear of not being liked, and I say no to social events or favors I truly don't wish to do. This helps me gain respect for setting clear boundaries, and conserves my energy so I have the stamina to accomplish things higher on my list.

Here is a guide that will help:

Step 1: Choose one fear to work on this week. It could be anything—public speaking, making decisions, or facing criticism—just make it on the easier side of the difficulty spectrum.

Step 2: Can you pinpoint the root cause of this fear? Have you always had it? Did it come on gradually or was there an event?

Step 3: Challenge your fear by planning one simple way you can confront this fear this week.

Step 4: Begin by taking one small action this week to practice confronting this fear.

Step 5: Praise and reward yourself for a job well done!

Some of Our Most Common Shared Fears

Beyond very specific fears like spiders or clowns, here are the ten most common fears I see in my work:

1. **Fear of the Unknown or Unfamiliar:** Many people fear not knowing what to expect or how events will unfold. They feel unable to control the outcomes or lack confidence in their skills to navigate an unsure future. This can cause people to avoid new experiences or anything that could potentially disrupt their routine. They may refuse to try new things or get involved in unfamiliar situations, leading to a lack of growth and development.

2. **Fear of Failure:** Being afraid of letting others down or not being successful, which can lead to an inability to take risks or try new things.

3. **Fear of Rejection:** Feeling rejected by others for any reason can be incredibly painful and leads many to avoid parts of their life (or experiences) that have the highest chance of rejection, which often pairs nicely with the next one on the list.

4. **Fear of Vulnerability:** Being vulnerable can make people feel exposed and unsafe, so they may put up walls to protect themselves from potential threats or rejections.

5. **Fear of Spontaneity:** Many people fear that if they lose control, their lives will become chaotic and unpredictable—and therefore even more terrifying! Predictability can feel safe, though it's a facade—we all live in a world that is, by nature, ever changing and chaotic.

6. **Fear of Loss:** Being paralyzed by the idea of losing something important, such as a job, home, relationship, or status.

7. **Fear of Making Mistakes:** Trying something new requires the courage to be wrong or to perform poorly at something.

When we're afraid to make mistakes, it can cause us to avoid trying new things or taking action altogether.

8. **Fear of Conflict:** Avoiding conflict or confrontations can feel safe in the short term, but many times it just delays decisions or makes situations worse.

9. **Fear of Abandonment:** Whether it's by choice or not, being left by our loved ones always hurts. However, letting this particular fear rule your life can prevent you from trusting others and creating the connections that would nourish you.

10. **Fear of Loneliness:** Everyone has their unique level of human interaction needs, from those who need lots of alone time to those who need constant companionship. However, when our fear of loneliness rules our life, it can keep us trapped in unhealthy behaviors and relationships.

drawn to murder mysteries and true crime—because they provide an opportunity for learning through the stories of others. We get to live vicariously through the characters and podcast hosts while we analyze and judge safely from the sidelines and think to ourselves: "I could see a serial killer from a mile away!"

True crime and (some) murder mysteries provide catharsis

True crime, complex mysteries, and horror can all trigger a fear-arousal response that can also allow us to play around with these difficult emotions. And when we come out on the other side, we can feel awash in the same relief sensations we'd have after our own real-life brushes with terror. In fact, that cathartic relief can be enough to draw us toward true crime, but so can the moments that come before the catharsis.

In the middle of any good true crime story, we recognize the moments that tell us things will turn out badly, though we don't know how. It's the same feeling we get in a haunted house, where we know something terrifying is about to happen but not what or when. In those moments, true crime lets us live this experience of terror vicariously through another person or character—while we remain safely tucked inside our favorite blanket. All we have to do to escape is press pause on the podcast or close the book. This pseudo-danger lets us safely explore some of the most dangerous spaces we can imagine.

WHEN YOU FEAR LOSING CONTROL

When we confine our fear to a late-night binge of *The Walking Dead* or a skydiving experience, we feel like we're in control. And oh, do humans love control. We need to put things in boxes, everything in its place, and answer every question. When something is misplaced or *can't* be placed, we're faced with the unknown. When we don't know how to respond to a situation, we can't predict how others will respond, so our sense of security is threatened.

Predictable routines, interactions, and outcomes make us feel safe because we believe we are in control. When we think we're losing that control, we translate that as a threat, which then leads to a fear response.

This fear of losing control can lead to an overwhelming feeling of spiraling out, which can result in us overanalyzing the situation and second-guessing ourselves. It's a common reaction when we feel unable to influence an outcome or are unprepared to succeed. But as unpleasant as it feels, it's normal. In fact, it's the result of hundreds of thousands of years of evolution. As humans, we rely on predictability to survive—certain foods growing at certain times of year, habits and routines that ensure everyone's needs are met, plus common norms, such as obeying traffic signals, all help keep us safe. And more, they present the illusion of control.

> When we think we're losing that control, we translate that as a threat, which then leads to a fear response.

COURAGE QUEST: Courage to Change

In the book *Junky*, American experimental novelist William S. Burroughs wrote, "When you stop growing, you start dying." Like it or not, this is true for every living organism, except maybe for Tardigrades —they've been on the earth for about 600 million years, can go 30 years without food or water, and are still tough as hell.

But change is hard, sometimes really hard. It can also be downright terrifying. And unexpected change, or even the hint of change, can send us plummeting into a fear spiral of feeling out of control or not good enough.

But change is good, even when it's difficult. Gobs of research on the mental and physical benefits of a "growth mindset" have been published since the mid-2000s when Stanford psychologist Carol Dweck first coined the term. However, not all of us see change as a welcome guest. Dive deeper into your own views and experiences on change with these prompts:

1. What strategies do you already have in place to navigate the big emotions that come with change? Do you feel they work well for you?

2. Looking back on your life, do you feel you've been someone who easily picked out those things you could change from those things that were out of your control?

3. Do you find change exciting and run toward it, or do you find it stressful and avoid it at all costs?

4. Can you describe the origin of your current mind chatter (your thoughts and feelings) when it comes to change?

5. Name one person in your life that you would nominate for the Best Change Navigator award. What makes this person worthy of such an accolade? Do you find similar traits in yourself? Would you even want to find similar traits in yourself? Why or why not?

So, when something unexpected happens we often see it as a loss of control. Unpredictability equals the unknown, and the unknown can be really scary.

WHEN YOU FEAR THAT YOU'RE NOT ENOUGH

The fear of not being enough can seriously mess with our sense of security. When was the last time you thought that, no matter how hard you tried, you wouldn't be able to meet the demands of life and that failure was a looming fire-breathing dragon? Last week? Yesterday? This morning? When we believe that we're unable to meet the demands of our world, we land in the bone-deep dread of inadequacy and insecurity, otherwise known as the feeling of not being (good, smart, pretty, wealthy, or thin) enough.

Modern life can feel like a gladiator match before a coliseum crowd, only the fight is against fear and rejection and disconnection instead of other gladiators and lions. And because our evolutionary roots for survival are firmly planted in community, it's completely natural that we fear the loss of our social status, success, power, and the love of others more than just about anything else. The fear of losing any of these can even surpass the fear of death. But these completely normal and natural fears don't have to be debilitating or block your path to belonging or happiness. You're not broken; there is nothing to fix. All you need are better tools to help make your journey faster and easier.

CHAPTER 3

Courage Is Learned

I learned that courage was not the
absence of fear, but the triumph over it.
—NELSON MANDELA

I n the summer of 2004, I was researching small mammals for my first biology master's degree, working in the Warner Mountains, an area of high desert plateaus in northeastern California. My study site was an eight-hour drive from where I lived, so it was next to impossible to get any free labor (aka friends) to come help me schlep hundreds of heavy aluminum small-mammal live traps through the sagebrush scrub in hundred-degree heat to collect field data. The study site was so remote, the nearest "town," called Likely, had a population of sixty-three and boasted one diner, one gas station, and a bar that hosted a hermaphroditic dog with only one eye. (Trust me when I say I'm not creative enough to make that up.)

Five days into my solo trip I was checking my traps to see if any mammals had found their way in, tempted by the treats they could pilfer before being gently examined and released, when I heard the unmistakable "pop-pop-pop" of gunshots echo across the plateau. My flinch-or-freeze instincts, which work faster than the more famous fight-or-flight fear reactions, had me dropping to my belly to hide as best I could while surrounded by miles of tiny gray bushes no taller than two feet.

As I tried to make myself as small as possible, my fight-or-flight response had time to kick in, and my brain quickly calculated the odds. This is when true terror began to set in. My mind made the immediate leap from gunshots to hunters to assuming most hunters were men to the deep, bone-rattling realization that I was an unarmed woman alone in the woods. And not just alone, but having to deal with a group of possibly dangerous men hundreds of miles away from anyone that might help if the bullets whizzing by were in fact meant for me and not a meaty deer.

In that moment, my mind went directly to every story I'd ever heard about what happens when women leave their house alone. Growing up in an American suburb trained me to be terrified of strange men and only abstractly afraid of bullets (I'm a child of the 1980s, so way before active shooter drills replaced dodgeball). In those first few seconds, my mind spun a thousand possible fates that I'd learned from a lifetime of cautionary tales about women who wore the wrong thing, said the wrong thing, or went somewhere they "shouldn't have."

Curled there in the dust, rapidly breathing in the sweet herbaceous scent of the California sage I was huddled under, I was far more terrified of what strange men might do to me than actually being shot.

I had learned to be more afraid of an imagined fate rooted in stories than the very real immediate danger of flying bullets.

Better Living Through Courage

Courage is one of the most important qualities we can cultivate in our lives. Living boldly allows us to face our fears, to stand up for ourselves and others, and to seize opportunities. Courage can also have a positive impact on our mental and emotional health, reducing stress and anxiety and increasing happiness.

It's the thing that allows you to overcome uncertainties and act in the face of fear. Engaging in brave behavior will also help you respond appropriately to risks in life and reach positive outcomes despite the discomfort we associate with feeling afraid.

Living boldly allows us to face our fears, to stand up for ourselves and others, and to seize opportunities.

COURAGE MAKES US STRONGER

Being courageous can build self-confidence. When we're faced with a difficult situation, it can be tempting to give up or to take the easy way out. However, if we choose to persevere through challenges, we often end up feeling proud of ourselves, which can boost self-confidence and help us feel even more capable in the future. Courage asks us to be vulnerable and to take risks, even when it feels gross to do so. As you accumulate more and more courageous acts, your confidence will naturally increase. With a track record of brave behavior under your belt, your feelings and beliefs about yourself *will* begin to change.

COURAGE MAKES US BETTER PROBLEM SOLVERS

When we're in a fear-arousal state, the problem-solving part of our brain, the prefrontal cortex, goes offline, making it hard, if not impossible, to create new, innovative solutions to problems both big and small. By stepping into courage as a practice, you can spend more of your day with your prefrontal cortex fully ready to support you.

Success seldom comes easy. It often requires taking risks and embracing uncertainty. Making brave choices can make it more likely that you pursue your dreams and seize the opportunities that arise. This is because you feel more confident about your abilities and are less likely to doubt yourself. Additionally, when you're confident in your tenacity to persevere, others see you as confident and comfortable in your own skin.

COURAGE REDUCES STRESS AND ANXIETY

By regularly embracing courage, you can increase your happiness, pride, and sense of safety. This feeling of empowerment then becomes the fuel to reach beyond your current limitations. When you actively work to navigate through your fear (what is colloquially referred to as stress), you feel more satisfied and content with your life, instead of regretting the opportunities you didn't seize.

COURAGE EMPOWERS THOSE AROUND YOU

Courage is contagious! Living with moxie is usually noticed by those in your life and can empower them to make courageous choices as well. It is especially important to lead by example if you're in a position of authority, such as a parent, coach, or manager. When people see you behaving bravely, they will be more likely to follow your lead. This can create a domino effect of courageous behavior with the potential to change an entire community or even the world.

When people see you behaving bravely, they will be more likely to follow your lead.

The Many Kinds of Courage

Every day, we encounter many different types of courage: the courage to stand up for what we believe in, despite opposition; the boldness to persist in the face of setbacks; and, of course, the bravery to face our fears. Each of these forms of courage is important in its own way. As you read what follows, consider which of these types of courage comes easily to you. Then think about those that speak to areas of your life in which you want to find more courage.

Bravery Break: Tapping into Courage

This neurohack is inspired by the Emotional Freedom Technique (EFT, also called psychological acupressure or tapping). There are many different ways to perform EFT, ranging from simple to complex. Here is a very simple, barebones tapping technique you can use when you're in the throes of a fear response:

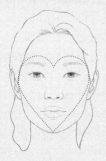

1. Take your two index fingers and place them gently between your eyebrows.

2. Start to gently tap the shape of a heart—with your left finger going to the left and your right going to the right. This heart should go around your eyebrows, down your temples, and under your cheeks, and your two fingers should meet again at your chin.

3. Once at your chin, drop them down to the center of your collarbone, then gently tap the two fingers away from each other, under the ridge of your collarbone, until you reach each shoulder.

Repeat this a few more times and notice if you begin to feel calmer and more relaxed.

Although research is still pretty new on the effectiveness of tapping, there are some promising early studies. In a 2013 study, veterans struggling with post-traumatic stress disorder (PTSD) reported a significant reduction in their psychological stress, with more than half of the EFT test group no longer fitting the official diagnostic criteria for PTSD after just thirty days of EFT coaching. More recently, in 2022 and 2023, healthcare professionals reported reduced anxiety and stress while experiencing an increase in self-esteem after integrating EFT into their daily lives.

PHYSICAL COURAGE

Physical courage, which is often how people think of all courage, involves bravery in the face of bodily danger or pain, even possible death. From acting to save a life in an emergency to skydiving for the first time, physical courage often requires quick thinking and decisive action. To strengthen this particular courage muscle, jump into activities that allow you to practice making the physically courageous choice in a *relatively* safe environment. Two of my favorites are scuba diving and rock climbing. Rock climbing in particular has the added benefit of rooting your focus in the present. I use it to help calm my racing, monkey mind, which loves to jump all over the place.

MORAL COURAGE

What do you stand for? How do you define right and wrong?

Moral courage is the ability to defend what you believe in, despite opposition, ridicule, or rejection. Moral courage is often associated with taking an ethical stand against something you know is wrong, despite potential negative consequences. But moral courage isn't just about standing up for your beliefs—it's also about recognizing difficult situations and doing the right thing even when it's hard or inconvenient.

This type of bravery can be seen in everyday life, from someone speaking out against a toxic work culture to someone standing up for their rights as a consumer. It can also happen on a large scale, such as civil rights leaders standing up to oppressive governments, or activists pushing for social change in society. But regardless of size or scope, moral courage requires you to take risks (which can be scary!) and put yourself in vulnerable positions to do what you believe is right.

How can you develop moral courage? The most important step is to be aware of your values and beliefs and develop the confidence to act on them. This means taking time to identify and reflect on what you believe in, to explore how you developed your beliefs, and then consider how they influence your behavior (see page 46). For me, the two hills I will absolutely die on are standing up for women's rights and access to education for all who desire it.

SOCIAL COURAGE

Whether it's in the classroom, around the dinner table, or at an event, there are times when you need to find your voice and use it. But this can be really hard, and we all experience moments when we struggle with how to communicate our thoughts effectively.

Studies suggest that people who display higher levels of social courage tend to be more successful in their professional lives as well as in their personal relationships.

Social courage is the ability to take risks, speak up, and engage in social situations with confidence, even in the face of possible social embarrassment, exclusion, or rejection. Studies suggest that people who display higher levels of social courage tend to be more successful in their professional lives as well as in their personal relationships.

Because social courage can be developed over time with practice, it's important to give yourself some leeway. This may not ever be your strong suit—and that is okay! You may also have strong social courage in some spaces but not others. (For example, I had no problem lecturing to a class of 400 biology students every Monday and Wednesday, but I struggled to find my voice when faced with my emotionally abusive caregiver.)

Of course, not everyone wants or needs to be a shiny social star, but if this is something you want to improve, there are some simple ways to cultivate stronger social courage. First, look for ways to understand the underlying fears that may be causing you to believe that your thoughts and opinions won't be respected or accepted by others. Can you identify an origin story attached to those beliefs?

Sometimes it can be easy to identify why you're holding back. For me, it was a lifetime of having my emotions and opinions disregarded by my mother that made me hesitant to share any new ones around others. However, don't fret if it takes more time and energy to tap into why you lack the bravery to speak up.

Then next comes the harder part: practice. By making a regular practice of offering an opinion during a meeting or discussion, you'll feel more relaxed and confident the more you do it. But don't worry—there are tools throughout this book to help!

INTELLECTUAL COURAGE

I love problem solving and creating novel solutions, so this flavor of courage is my favorite. At its core, intellectual courage involves challenging your own beliefs as well as the assumptions and ideas of others. It involves questioning established norms and thinking critically about the theories and concepts presented to you in order to build an informed opinion. Intellectual courage requires a deep understanding of yourself and your abilities. It takes confidence in your ideas and the strength to stand up for what you believe in. Intellectual courage also requires resilience, or the ability to keep going despite criticism, bad decisions, and setbacks.

Self-doubt, fear of failure, and hesitation can all stand in the way of making brave decisions. The worry of being wrong or making mistakes can be challenging to move through since so many of us have been conditioned to think everything must be perfect before we can move ahead. Being from Silicon Valley, I've used the Big Tech mantra of "Move Fast and Break Things" and "Fail Fast, Fail Often" as guiding stars in my professional work.

Self-doubt, fear of failure, and hesitation can all stand in the way of making brave decisions.

My personal definition of "Move Fast and Break Things" is "Don't be afraid to experiment, don't be afraid to play, don't be afraid to do what others won't." Having a strong sense of intellectual courage gave me a well of power to tap into in order to study an area—non-clinical fear and everyday daring—that wasn't the focus of many scientists. Intellectual courage allowed me the fortitude to share my findings with the world, on stage and in this book!

My second-favorite Silicon Valley saying, "Fail Fast, Fail Often," I define as an iterative process of "create, experiment, repeat." Practicing this approach allows me to disconnect my self-worth from the inevitable failures that come with doing something new.

"Fail Fast, Fail Often" also reminds me to move past the mental framing that failure is embarrassing and into the mindset that failure can be quite beneficial. Failing allows us to learn from our mistakes, practice resilience, and develop strategies for future success. Even though it can still hurt—a lot—practicing failure not only strengthens our intellectual courage muscles but helps us become more comfortable with risk-taking across all aspects of our life.

EMOTIONAL COURAGE

One of my least favorite types, emotional courage is why I began studying fear and courage in the first place. Being raised by an emotionally abusive mother who ruled her house through fear made me absolutely terrible at understanding or expressing my emotions.

Emotional courage involves being open to feeling and expressing a full range of human emotions. It can also be defined as the ability to confront and manage difficult emotional experiences, such as fear, uncertainty, guilt, shame, anger, and sadness. Emotional courage is the willingness to feel uncomfortable feelings while still taking action. It's not about being fearless or avoiding unpleasant emotions; rather, it's about recognizing that these emotions are a natural part of human existence but choosing to move forward despite the discomfort.

Having emotional courage is an essential skill that allows us to take risks and live authentically. It gives us the confidence to express our truths and face our vulnerabilities, resulting in more happiness, more freedom, and more loving relationships. This book was born of my desire to strengthen my own emotional courage because I was tired of feeling like I was experiencing a black-and-white life while others lived in full color. I wanted to learn how to tap into my inner strength and make brave choices despite feeling scared or uncertain.

EXISTENTIAL COURAGE

Whenever someone asked me how the writing of this book was "going," I'd respond, "Oh, you know, just another day of existential dread." Although I was joking (mostly), feeling anxious about what the future holds and the impact of your decisions on that future is a normal part of being human. The decisions we make, from big to tiny, can drastically alter everything, and it's easy to descend into the depths of indecision when the waters get rough. Or if it's a Tuesday. Both are perfectly valid reasons to feel existential dread.

So, if existential dread exists, existential courage must be a thing, too. And luckily it is! "Existential courage" refers to the courage of regularly choosing the least familiar path instead of taking the well-trodden one. Without this kind of daring, you may become that friend who dates one hundred different versions of the same guy, the one who constantly says yes to different flavors of their familiar past.

Existential courage refers to the courage of regularly choosing the least familiar path instead of taking the well-trodden one.

Developing a sense of existential courage can help you become more comfortable with uncertainty because you know that, regardless of what happens in the future, you have the inner strength to keep going. Existential courage refers to your ability to confront difficult situations and make decisions despite feeling overwhelmed or confused about what lies ahead. Rather than succumbing to societal pressures or simply following trends, those of us with existential courage make decisions based on our core values.

COURAGE QUEST: Values

Ask yourself the following questions and then jot down your responses to begin to articulate your core values:

What makes you feel fulfilled?

....

....

What do you believe is necessary for leading a meaningful life?

....

....

Where are you willing to compromise?

....

....

What do you believe in and stand for?

....

....

What makes you feel most alive and fulfilled as a person?

....

....

What are your highest priorities and passions?

....

....

What do you see as your calling in life?

....

....

Do most of your daily actions align with your core values?

....

....

Core Values and Courage

Courage is strongest at the intersection of your most important values, taking appropriate action, and the ability to push through the discomfort of fearful emotions.

We all have core values that shape how we make decisions and therefore how we live our lives. These core values are woven into your life's purpose, who you are, and who you want to become. Core values are the beliefs or principles that drive your behavior, both positive and negative, and they often reflect your upbringing, education, culture, and life experiences. When it comes to living with more courage and less fear, your core values can provide a powerful compass to keep you motivated and on track.

Core values are part of who you are, what matters to you, and what motivates your decisions. Discovering your own isn't as easy as thinking about your personality traits, the values you were taught, or your career goals. The process requires mindfulness, deep reflection, and vulnerability.

Purpose leads to persistence, and visiting and revisiting our values helps ensure we have the fuel to keep moving forward, even on the rockiest of roads.

WHAT DO YOU VALUE?

Years ago, there was a popular social post with a ten-by-ten-letter word search accompanied by a message that said, "The first three words you see are the three things most important to you." Hidden among the random letters were three words that popped out for me: *love, knowledge,* and *power.* I still remember the post because that silly word search game wasn't wrong! Although love and knowledge were easy ones to own, I felt a little dirty picking power as my third word.

But core values are not inherently right or wrong. Power isn't necessarily good or bad—it's what people do with power that is more important. Power can drive people to commit terrible atrocities or to provide education, food, clean water, healthcare, and affordable housing to communities that need it.

So, as you experiment with the word search method, treat it as a game. Set a timer for two minutes and go through the list below, choosing every word that resonates with you but without deciding if it's "good" or "bad." Then whittle your list down to a top ten, then a top five. I recommend using a timer because it's easy to overthink this and want your first list to be perfect. It won't be, and you can adjust it anytime. In fact, the best way to find your truest core values is to repeat the exercise, since it can take a few tries to filter out what we think we "should" have as our core values versus the ones we actually have. To download a printable copy of this list if you'd rather circle your favorites, go to https://marypoffenroth.com /bravenewyou.

Kindness	Joy	Diversity
Respect	Positivity	Maturity
Compassion	Flexibility	Freedom
Integrity	Confidence	Spontaneity
Honesty	Service to others	Faith
Humility	Appreciation of	Appreciation of
Generosity	beauty	nature
Responsibility	Wonder and awe	Living in the
Gratitude	Self-discovery	moment
Selflessness	Tolerance	Achievement
Open-mindedness	Passion	Adaptability
Patience	Adventure	Authenticity
Forgiveness	Optimism	Ambition
Empathy	Trustworthiness	Winning
Perseverance	Balance	Balance
Loyalty	Peacefulness	Justice
Dependability	Gratitude for life	Belonging
Creativity	Humor	Collaboration

Commitment	Modesty	Uniqueness
Community	Love	Composure
Connection	Organization	Vitality
Curiosity	Patriotism	Depth
Dignity	Being a parent	Structure
Equality	Power	Free-thinking
Fairness	Unity	Worthiness
Family	Pride	Fitness
Wealth	Resilience	Goodness
Friendship	Resourcefulness	Beauty
Fun	Risk	Inventiveness
Legacy	Thrift	Learning
Harmony	Preparedness	Variety
Hope	Time	Moderation
Independence	Solitude	Prosperity
Safety	Truth	Stability
Growth	Wisdom	Playfulness
Health	Sensuality	Tidiness
Leadership	Affection	
Leisure	Charity	

Another way to use this word search is to consider the list above with the following prompts:

Think of three people you admire and select two traits you find most desirable in them. These are most likely traits that you either have or truly want to have.

Reflecting on your biggest successes, which specific values from above led you to them? What about your biggest failures?

Defining your core values can give you the clarity and confidence to set and pursue goals that will bring meaning and purpose to your life. Think about how your current lifestyle reflects your values. What do they look like when you put them into practice? When we align our behaviors with our values, it becomes easier to step into a space of courage and maintain our motivation for change.

Attachment Styles

We are wired for connection. Research shows that deep, trusting relationships with others make us naturally more courageous and less afraid. However, it's incredibly difficult for many of us to form meaningful relationships due to our early life experiences. A concept rooted in psychology, attachment styles are patterns of how we behave in relationships. Our attachment styles, largely established in infancy and influenced by our caregivers, profoundly impact our thoughts, feelings, actions, and ability to connect to others as adults.

Developed in the 1950s by British psychologist John Bowlby, the theory behind attachment styles proposes that infants develop an emotional bond with their primary caregiver—usually their mother—early in life. This bond is based on the infant's need for security, comfort, and protection from danger. Bowlby suggested that if an infant's needs were met consistently during their early years, they would develop a sense of security that would carry over into adulthood, making it easier for them to form healthy relationships later in life.

The first step toward changing our personal relationship stories is to recognize the attachment pattern we've inherited from our caregivers.

Building on Bowlby's attachment theory, psychologist Mary Ainsworth identified three attachment styles: secure, anxious-avoidant (usually referred to as just "avoidant"), and anxious-resistant (traditionally referred to as just "anxious"). Subsequent research would add a fourth: disorganized, or fearful-avoidant. Those with secure attachment styles tend to live more courageous and less fearful lives. But even if you left childhood with an insecure attachment style, you can transform how you connect to others through understanding and practice.

Since understanding your attachment style is the first step toward reaping the courage-building benefits of feeling secure, I've

COURAGE QUEST:
Reshaping Your Attachment Style

Now that you've identified those values that are important to you, it's time to imagine your ideal relationship. Start with one single type of relationship: professional, romantic, friendship, or even the relationship you have with yourself, and answer the following:

1. List five nice-to-have values (wants) and five deal-breaker values (needs) that must exist in this ideal relationship.

2. Describe why you feel that having a relationship centered on those values would be healthier than the relationships you have now.

What support or skills do you need to go from where you're at to where you want to be?

created nicknames (see sidebar) to help you easily remember them, since understanding attachment styles can also help you understand, and more deeply connect to, the emotions and behaviors of those in your life. And though you can get a professional assessment from a licensed therapist or counselor, it really isn't needed unless your struggles in this area need professional support so you can thrive.

To begin, think about important past relationships (both romantic and platonic). Before you go through the list, have just one important relationship at the top of your mind to experiment with. For this first exercise, it doesn't matter whether things turned out well or not; just don't choose a relationship that still has too much unresolved emotion attached to it, which can make it hard for you to have enough distance to see what patterns emerge.

After you've read through the attachment styles, take a wider view of your life and think about the last few years as a whole. Are there certain types of people that make you feel safe? Do certain situations cause anxiety for you? Do certain conversations bring up feelings of insecurity?

Also, it's essential that you know you are not stuck with the type of attachment style you developed in childhood or even the one you have right now. It's not automatic and no wand waving will change things overnight, but we do have control over our destinies.

The Attachment Style Cheat Sheet

Start with a quick look at the types below, then look for longer explanations to follow:

- **The Well-Anchored (Secure attachment style):** You have a track record of long-lasting relationships built on trust and vulnerability. You're good at conflict resolution and have no problem sharing thoughts and feelings or seeking comfort from others.

- **The Chaser (Anxious attachment style):** Looking back on your life's previous relationships, you can see a pattern of clingy behavior rooted in your fears of abandonment and rejection. You constantly doubt your partner's love and commitment, which drives you to hang on tighter or chase after them. There is a good chance you grew up in a household where you got conflicting messages from your primary caregivers, which led to a lot of confusion about how to regulate your big emotions. You may have also experienced frightening or chaotic events at a young age.

- **The Runaway (Avoidant attachment style):** Due to moments of your life ruled by being hurt or rejected, you prefer to be hyper-independent. You desire connection but at the same time fear intimacy and find yourself running away when things get too emotionally close. You have a strong sense of independence and find it easy to distrust others. There's a good chance you grew up not having your emotional or physical needs met by your primary caregivers, forcing you to grow up quickly in order to survive.

- **The Hot and Cold (Disorganized attachment style):** You're a little bit chaser, a little bit runaway. You find yourself oscillating between running toward and away from partners and have been accused of sending mixed signals by others. Looking back, you can see that you grew up in a household where expressing big emotions was frowned on by neglectful, chaotic, or overly demanding primary caregivers.

The first step toward changing our personal relationship stories is to recognize the attachment pattern we've inherited from our caregivers. The next step is to understand the patterns of behavior that show up in our relationships with friends, colleagues, and significant others as a result so we can work on reshaping them.

SECURE: THE WELL-ANCHORED

Do you find that your relationships tend to be long-lasting, characterized by trust, good conflict resolution, an ability to effectively seek comfort from a partner, and a willingness to be vulnerable in sharing thoughts and feelings? Then look at you, big winner! You have a secure attachment style!

Those with secure attachment styles tend to be better equipped to cope with fear or stress. Feeling secure as a child leads more easily to being an adult who feels comfortable expressing their emotions without fear of judgment or rejection.

If you left childhood with this type of attachment style, there's a very good chance that you had a dependable, loving relationship with a primary caregiver who responded promptly to your physical and emotional needs, consistently offering comfort, warmth, and love. Typically, this has allowed you to be more successful at forming meaningful relationships because trust and communication come more naturally to you.

TEAM INSECURE: ANXIOUS, AVOIDANT, AND DISORGANIZED

If the secure attachment style doesn't reflect the current you, don't worry! No matter what style you identify with, you can grow toward a secure attachment style with knowledge, insight, and action. Insecure attachment styles develop when a child experiences conflicting messages from their primary caregiver or has been exposed to frightening or chaotic events during childhood. This can lead to confusion about how to regulate challenging emotions (especially fear) and difficulty in forming healthy relationships.

All forms of insecure attachments come with challenges, but understanding why they exist is key to overcoming them and fostering healthier interpersonal relationships going forward. We all yearn to be seen, heard, and understood, to love and be loved in return. So, let's begin with increasing your knowledge and insights about the three styles on "team insecure."

Anxious: The chaser

If you tend to grasp overly tightly to another because you're afraid they'll slip away, constantly doubt your partner's love and commitment, and are terrified of abandonment or rejection, then you're most like a chaser. Chasers are constantly pursuing the love they never got as a child and hold others in such a fierce bear hug that they can feel overwhelmed or stifled.

This attachment style is deeply rooted in fears of abandonment and rejection stemming from caregivers who were easily overwhelmed or made children responsible for their adult emotions. As adults, chasers often have difficulty trusting other people or forming close relationships, as deep feelings of unworthiness and insecurity cause them to become overly dependent on their partner for emotional support.

Since this interaction pattern develops when a child has had to navigate unpredictable parenting from an emotionally unavailable caregiver, chasers tend to be highly attuned to their partner's feelings and emotions while simultaneously having difficulty controlling their own. Chasers also tend to feel insecure in relationships and worry about being rejected or abandoned, often seeking constant reassurance or validation from their partner, leading them to become clingy or overly dependent.

Having an anxious attachment style can have a major impact on relationships, both romantic and platonic alike, as it can make one highly sensitive to criticism and desperate for approval. Chasers may feel jealous or suspicious if their partner spends time away from them, even if there is no logical reason for these feelings. With an intense need for closeness and connection in their relationships, chasers may find it difficult to participate in activities without their partner due to separation anxiety or fear of being alone. In some cases, these behaviors push others away, which can morph into a fear of the other person walking away that is so intense that they sacrifice their own needs and desires just to avoid conflict.

Avoidant: The runaway

When others get emotionally close, does running away feel like the safest option for you?

Avoidant attachment styles come from having to grow up too soon. Were you expected to be independent and, basically, raise yourself when you were far too young? Perhaps those who were meant to be your protectors were slow to respond to even your most basic needs, and maybe even punished you for needing anything at all. When you did share your desire for connection, warmth, and love, you were routinely met with rejection, so you began to equate safety with hyper-independence.

After years of not having their needs met, runaways internalize the message that it's better to be alone than emotionally vulnerable, making closeness and intimacy uncomfortable or even terrifying. This messaging can be so deeply ingrained that it can feel incredibly dangerous when others do try to love them, causing them to flee when a relationship begins to get too emotionally close. Runaways learn to cope with difficult emotions and situations by shutting down their feelings and avoiding closeness with others, focusing only on their own needs and goals. Sometimes categorized as having "commitment issues" in adult romantic relationships, runaways often struggle with trust, making it incredibly difficult to share thoughts and feelings with others.

Runaways may also have difficulty expressing themselves openly, making them appear distant or unapproachable to others even when they long for connection. During childhood, runaways learn that reaching out for help or expressing emotional needs will not be met with positive reinforcement. This can look like truly neglectful parenting, but also presents as being raised with such impossibly high standards for external greatness, like grades or athletics, that there was no space to express emotions. They may also find themselves engaging in patterns of distancing behaviors, such as dismissing compliments or disregarding the needs of others.

Disorganized: The hot and cold

When reading about anxious and avoidant attachment styles, did you see yourself as a little bit of both? Oscillating between running toward and running away from close relationships in a seemingly endless cycle of chase, flee, chase? If so, then you probably best align with the disorganized style of attachment that I call "hot and cold."

This is the attachment style that I most align with, and that caused me the most misery over the years without my even knowing it. Looking back on my relationships, I can see my pattern of desperately wanting closeness while simultaneously being anxious or mistrustful of friends, partners, or colleagues. I was both afraid of losing them *and* of them getting too close.

Disorganized attachment presents as more of a combination of anxious and avoidant styles when someone oscillates between being clingy and distant. Those like me who exhibit a disorganized attachment often struggle to regulate their emotions because of past trauma or neglect. Intense bouts of grief, anger, guilt, or shame related to early childhood experiences lead hot and cold people to become easily overwhelmed by intense emotions since they never learned how to navigate them properly in childhood. Because of this intense emotionality, people who have a disorganized attachment style often behave in unpredictable or contradictory ways, which leads to confusion and difficulty in forming connections. For example, hot and cold individuals may move away from their partner during difficult conversations yet still seek closeness afterward. This can lead to confusion and frustration for both involved in the relationship.

Hot and colds are forged in similar childhood environments as those from anxious or avoidant groups, where a lack of emotional security leads to developing maladaptive coping strategies. They may try hard not to express any negative emotions so as not to push away potential partners from fear they will be rejected if they do so. As a result, they may resort to manipulative tactics such as lying or withholding information in order to keep partners close without having to confront them about their emotional needs directly.

Understanding attachment styles helps us better understand how past experiences shape the past and present behavior of ourselves and those around us. It can also offer insight into how we emotionally react to our internal and external experiences. We can then use this information to become more confident in our ability to form lasting relationships by building trust through open communication rather than relying solely on intuition or past experience.

CHAPTER 4

The Science of Fear Is Powerful

Increasing the strength of our minds is the only way
to reduce the difficulty of life.
—MOKOKOMA MOKHONOANA

Behind every daring feat or act of survival are complex neurological processes. Our brains are hardwired for fear precisely so that we can learn to better manage it the next time. A basic understanding of how our fear-arousal responses work can make it easier to employ the upcoming tools and strategies to manage your fear and grow your courage.

By understanding the connections between different hormones, anatomical structures, neurotransmitters, and other physiological processes associated with fear, you can gain a next-level understanding of how your body responds when faced with difficult situations. Having a sense of these processes will help boost your awareness so you can be better prepared to cope when the inevitable stresses of life appear.

And, while I believe having a foundational understanding of the science behind fear and courage is crucial to squeezing the most value from this book, I'm also a science communicator, so I want to make science enjoyable and accessible for all.

And for some, that means skipping the foundational science. If that's you, no judgments, but I would ask you to at least take in the basics before moving on.

The Foundations of Fear and Courage: The Nervous System

Our nervous system is responsible for everything from basic physical functions to our most complex thoughts and emotions, including fear and courage.

It is split into the central nervous system (CNS) and the peripheral nervous system (PNS). The CNS contains the brain and spinal cord, controlling actions and responses. The PNS transfers information between the CNS and the body. Think of the CNS as a computer, while the PNS is the connecting cables.

The PNS consists of two subsystems: the somatic nervous system (responsible for carrying out actions we choose to do, like speaking or waving) and the autonomic nervous system (responsible for all the automatic processes that keep us alive, like digestion). It is within the autonomic subsystem that we find the keys to fear and courage. Working in opposition of each other, where only one can be in control at a time, we have the sympathetic nervous system, the "gas pedal," and the parasympathetic nervous system, the "brakes."

When your brain perceives a threat that it needs to act on, the sympathetic nervous system (the gas pedal) takes over to prepare your body for things like fight or flight. When life is calm and we can return to rest, the parasympathetic nervous system (the brakes) takes over so that the body can deal with all the normal functions such as digesting food and making new cells that were put on hold while we dealt with whatever threat was before us. Most of your day should be spent with the parasympathetic nervous system (the brakes) in control, as the sympathetic nervous system (the gas pedal) should only be used in emergencies.

However, in our fast-paced modern lives, too often we get stuck in gas pedal mode, which leaves us feeling drained and exhausted.

The Nervous System: A Very Short Introduction

Understanding how fear works in your body begins with the central nervous system (CNS) and peripheral nervous system (PNS), which contain two subsystems: the somatic nervous system, responsible for voluntary actions, and the autonomic nervous system, which controls vital background processes like digestion.

The autonomic nervous system can be further broken down into two parts: the sympathetic nervous system (or gas pedal, which helps us prepare for danger) and the parasympathetic nervous system (or brakes, which helps us restore equilibrium after a stressful encounter).

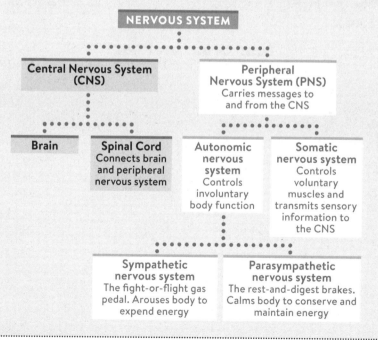

The Amygdala and the Prefrontal Cortex: The Yin and Yang of Fear Arousal

The two major power players in your brain when it comes to fear and courage are the amygdala and the prefrontal cortex.

THE AMYGDALA: THE EMOTIONAL SMOKE DETECTOR

Upon encountering a possible threat, your brain sends a distress signal to your amygdala, a pair of almond-shaped structures deep in your brain's center. Commonly referred to as "The Fear Center," which is a bit of an oversimplification, the amygdala will trigger a cascade of physiological responses if the possible threat is upgraded to an actual one. If so, the amygdala sets off the chain of reactions called the fear-arousal response, flooding your body with adrenaline, resulting in a racing heart, faster breathing, and sharpened senses.

Your Brain on Fear

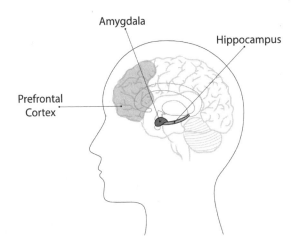

Amygdala

Hippocampus

Prefrontal Cortex

Your amygdala still operates in an ancient and binary way, which means it doesn't know how to best protect you in our modern world. Think of your amygdala as an overprotective best friend who threatens all your partners with bodily harm "if they ever hurt you." This friend has the best intentions—keeping you safe!—but also tends to overreact and can cause lots of unnecessary drama. Another way to think of your amygdala is as a smoke detector, constantly monitoring for danger. Finally, try to remember that there is no nuanced in-between for your amygdala—you are either safe or in danger.

THE PREFRONTAL CORTEX: THE LOGICAL COMMAND CENTER

Conversely, courage relies heavily on the prefrontal cortex (PFC)—a part of the brain associated with higher cognitive functions like decision making, problem solving, logic, and regulating behavior and emotions. The PFC works by controlling our impulses and helping us make better judgments about risks or predicting outcomes for future actions.

When you feel fear but decide to act anyway, your prefrontal cortex helps override the fear response initiated by your amygdala, allowing you to move forward courageously.

Recent research has shown the PFC to be uniquely active when we're solving problems that require creativity and innovation. This suggests that our PFCs play an important role in our ability to come up with new ideas and find unique solutions to problems.

But as our fear arousal goes up, our creative abilities go down, because the actions of our amygdala impair our PFC's ability to function at full capacity. In fact, many experts say fear is the biggest threat to individual creativity. Even though engaging in creative tasks has been shown to decrease stress, depression, and anxiety, fear changes our brains and impairs our ability to create new solutions, do our best work, and carry out those new solutions instead of forever practicing old ones.

These two areas of your brain function together to help you navigate the world safely, by recognizing potential danger and responding to it accordingly. In moments of fear, it can feel like there's a tug-of-war happening in your brain, with the amygdala shouting "Danger!" and the prefrontal cortex saying, "Let's think this through." By consistently engaging with your fears in a safe, managed way and using the neurohacks in this book, you can train your amygdala to overreact less and strengthen your prefrontal cortex courage connections, helping you become more confident and less fearful.

Another way to think of your amygdala is as a smoke detector, constantly monitoring for danger.

Supporting Fear and Courage in the Limbic System

The limbic system is often referred to as the "emotional brain" or the "seat of emotions," a simplification of what is really a distributed network of brain structures that regulate emotions, motivation, and memory, composed of the hypothalamus, amygdala, hippocampus, and other subcortical (i.e., beneath the cortex) structures. In addition, the limbic system regulates crucial functions, including wakefulness, attention, hunger, stress, and sex. It also plays a role in emotional processing and memory formation.

Once you understand that you're hardwired to experience fear, you can begin to internalize that fear is not a moral failing. Rather, it's a complex response system with multiple pathways, dozens of hormones, and various parts of the brain involved. By exploring how the limbic system functions, you can become more aware of how your emotional states are not fully within your control or if your experience is not exactly what others would wish. Understanding the limbic system gives us a better sense of how our bodies distribute the responsibilities of managing fear and courage.

The hippocampus: The memory maestro

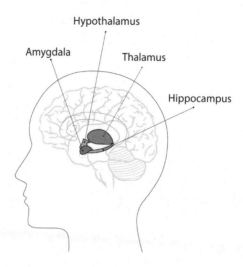

Hypothalamus

Amygdala

Thalamus

Hippocampus

This seahorse-shaped structure helps process long-term memory and emotional responses. It works with the amygdala, helping form emotions such as fear, happiness, or anger. It also plays a role in memory formation and spatial navigation, helping you remember how to get from one place to another.

Located in the brain's temporal lobe, the hippocampus is especially important for forming declarative memories (i.e., memories that can be explicitly stated or recalled), such as facts and events. When the amygdala and the hippocampus interact, you can develop learned fears. Once something has scared you in the past, the hippocampus latches on to that memory

Once you understand that you're hardwired to experience fear, you can begin to internalize that fear is not a moral failing.

and doesn't let it go. The hippocampus has the best of intentions, of course—it doesn't want you to make the same dangerous mistake again. But sometimes your hippocampus is the one making the mistake. How? By keeping you afraid of something that isn't really all that dangerous.

The hippocampus is one of the very few brain regions where, even later in life, new neurons can be made, a process called neurogenesis. Most of the brain's growth and development ends when you're around twenty-five years old, but with the help of the brain-derived neurotrophic factor (BDNF), we can continue to heal and grow neurons throughout our life.

The thalamus: The relay station

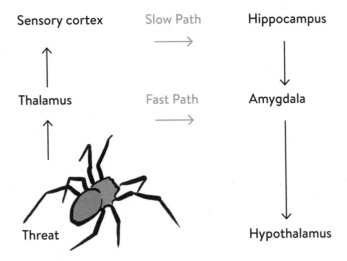

When examining the impact of fear on the brain, a key player to consider is our "sensory relay station"—the thalamus. Serving as a kind of hub, the thalamus transmits sensory information from our body to the appropriate areas in our brain.

When a fear-inducing event occurs, the sensory information (what we see, hear, touch, and so forth) enters the brain via the thalamus. The thalamus, in turn, sends this data along two separate pathways. The "fast path," a quicker but less precise pathway, sends the information straight to the amygdala, ushering in the immediate fear response. The "slow path," a slower yet more thorough route, takes the information to the sensory cortex where it's analyzed in detail before being sent to the amygdala. It allows us to consciously recognize and understand the source of the fear. This dual-route system is fundamental to the manifestation of our fear responses.

Interestingly, both pathways work simultaneously, so we may react to a potential threat before we're fully aware of what it is, which helps increase our chances of surviving peril. Understanding the role of the thalamus in processing fear helps us appreciate the complexity of our fear responses and the physiological aspects that can enhance or diminish them.

The hypothalamus: The thermostat

The hypothalamus releases hormones and regulates body functions such as temperature, thirst, and hunger, and is a key player in our fear-arousal response. When you perceive something as threatening, your amygdala triggers the hypothalamus, which then springs into action, initiating a series of physical responses that prepare you for a fight-or-flight response. This includes accelerating your breathing and heart rate, dilating your pupils, and slowing the digestive process. At the same time, it releases stress-related hormones like adrenaline and cortisol, to prepare your body to respond to the perceived danger.

The Chemicals of Courage

Understanding how neurotransmitters like dopamine and serotonin affect our experiences of fear, courage, and resilience is an essential part of tackling our fears. Establishing their role also helps dismantle the years (so many years) of shame and social conditioning that compelled us to see fear as a moral failing instead of the normal functioning of the human body.

By diving deeper into neurotransmitters, the chemicals that relay messages between neurons in our brains, we start to understand the vital role they play in mood, memory, and many other brain functions.

Epinephrine: It's 3:00 a.m. and you hear a noise downstairs. Your heart starts to race, the hair on your neck stands up, and you start to sweat. You feel like you might vomit. You're paralyzed by fear.

Once your brain perceives the threat, it sends a signal to your adrenal glands to release epinephrine, a neurotransmitter *and* a hormone, into the bloodstream. Epinephrine, also known as adrenaline, then binds to receptors on cells throughout your body, preparing you for full battle mode.

With your sympathetic nervous system activated, your heart rate and breathing speed up so that more oxygen can be delivered to your muscles. Blood is redirected from your digestive organs so more of it can flow to your limbs. Your pupils dilate so that you can see better, and you start to sweat in order to cool down your overheating muscles. You're now alert and laser focused. Epinephrine has given you the courage to face danger head-on (or the strength to run away as fast as you can!).

Norepinephrine: Think of norepinephrine as epinephrine's assistant. In response to a stress trigger, norepinephrine is released and travels to the brain, where it activates the sympathetic nervous system. The result leads to an increase in heart rate, blood pressure, and respiration. With the accompanying increases in blood sugar, you're prepared for action with increased alertness, focus, and attention.

Glutamate: When you experience fear, the amygdala sends signals to the hypothalamus to increase glucocorticoid hormones, leading to an increase in glutamate release. This surge in glutamate causes the body to release adrenaline and cortisol, which prepares your body to either face your fears or run away from them. However, this response can also be harmful when it occurs in response to things not actually dangerous, leading to glutamate playing a role in depression and anxiety.

Dopamine: Dopamine helps you feel pleasure and motivates you to repeat behaviors that lead to that feeling. It is sometimes called the "happy chemical" because it's involved in activities the brain finds pleasurable—including eating, sex, and exercise. When you engage in these activities, your brain releases dopamine. So it has a huge impact on our ability to feel empowered, energized, and optimistic. Basically, as your dopamine levels increase you feel better, even amazing!

But as your dopamine levels decrease, you feel continually worse and even out of control in your life. And since dopamine also affects your working memory and executive function, it can cause you to perform poorly on tests of cognitive ability and feel apathetic when your levels of it are low. In fact, dopamine is such a powerful force on how you feel every day that dopamine replacement therapy is a powerful treatment option for many battling clinical depression.

In terms of fear and courage, your brain releases dopamine when you encounter a potential threat to help you assess the situation and decide how to respond. This rush of dopamine gives you the energy and focus you need to face danger. In other words, without dopamine you wouldn't be able to muster up the courage to face your fears.

Serotonin: Serotonin plays a prominent role in regulating mood and emotion by influencing the release of other neurotransmitters, like dopamine and norepinephrine. It's often referred to as the "love" or "bonding" chemical when its levels are high. But when too much serotonin floods the brain you'll feel overstimulated, leading to problems like hallucinations or insomnia (which is why the drug MDMA helps ravers dance until dawn).

On the flip side, consistently low levels of serotonin have been linked to depression, anxiety, and other mental health conditions. In terms of fear, mounting evidence suggests that serotonin plays a major role in not just how we experience fear and courage but also how those memories are processed. Your diet and how much cxercise and sunlight you're getting can also affect your daily serotonin levels. It's all part of the complex equation of why you feel good when you exercise, eat right, and get some sun.

Oxytocin: At the heart of our connections with others is oxytocin, which is released when you participate in any social bonding activity, from spooning with your partner to cuddling a puppy or laughing with friends, or even a not-so-great social interaction like being bullied by your boss.

Although oxytocin is famously known as the "love" hormone, promoting feelings of connecting, safety, and bonding, it's actually more general than that. Oxytocin strengthens our memories of *all* social interactions, good and bad.

You can thank oxytocin for part of the complex reason why you still cringe, even twenty years later, when you recall the entire class laughing at you during your graduation picnic. New research has shown a darker side to the previously coined "happy" hormone, one that forces us to recall long-past stressful experiences with vibrant clarity, and that can help reinforce similar fear triggers in the future.

Your Brain and Body on Fear: Putting It All Together

Would you get on a sailboat with a captain who had no idea how the engine, sails, or rudder worked?

If there is one thing to remember from all the science presented in this chapter it is this: Our physical and emotional states are connected.

My answer would be, "Hell no." I want my health, safety, and enjoyment looked after by a steward who knew what they were doing and had at least a cursory knowledge of how all the bits and pieces worked to get me from point A to point B.

Seems pretty basic, yet we're born into incredibly complex bodies with little to no instruction on how things work or, in other words, how to expertly sail through the rough seas of life.

If there is one thing to remember from all the science presented in this chapter it is this: Our physical and emotional states are connected. When we understand the how and the why of our brains, we can use that knowledge to make decisions that reflect our true desires. Through science, we gain a better understanding of how to cultivate courage and find success in the face of fear.

There is a degree of will and choice, but much of our emotional experiences are driven by our biology. Not to say this gives you carte blanche to run around behaving like an awful person, but understanding this distribution of responsibility allows us to let go of the blame-and-shame game, building empathy for ourselves and everyone we meet.

There is no one-size-fits-all approach to cultivating courage. Everyone has different needs and goals, so it's essential to experiment and find the approach that works best for you.

You're the captain of your ship! What new future do you want to sail to next?

PART TWO

The Cages
of Fear

CHAPTER 5

Biological Fear: The Cages We're Born Into

When you're scared, but you still do it anyway, that's brave.
—NEIL GAIMAN, *CORALINE*

Recently, I took my freshman biology class out for a teaching hike. We began the day gathered in a circle to chat about what we would do on the trail. As I spoke, a small snake the size of a straw slithered through the center of our circle. I immediately noticed our little friend and mentally identified its species but deliberately didn't mention its presence. I didn't want to startle anyone into hurting the snake or themselves.

Some of my savvier students noticed the snake and pointed it out to their friends. Eventually, I had to address the "snake" in the room. I assured my students there was nothing to worry about and recommended they just stay still and let it pass, allowing them to assume it was a harmless snake.

It was, in fact, a highly venomous juvenile northern Pacific rattlesnake (*Crotalus oreganus*).

Adult rattlesnakes can modulate their behavior, having a greater ability to consider the benefits of wasting venom, a costly resource, on a bite. However, juveniles, just like an overly tired toddler, haven't learned modulation yet, so will bite with full venom first and ask questions later, making them far more dangerous.

At that moment, the biggest threat was how my students reacted to the snake, not the snake itself. Although they can look scary and are potentially lethal, snakes are animals that just want to survive. Like us, they will react when threatened but would much rather go about their business without getting into a fight. Wild animals, even apex predators, know that every altercation carries with it a probability of death, so it's best to avoid a fight rather than risk losing one.

Had my students reacted to the very small chance of getting bit instead of the reality of a tiny snake cruising by on its day, that small chance could have become a big reality. Our biology wouldn't be to blame because most primates, including humans, have evolved an ingrained fear of snakes. What would be blameworthy is how we chose to react to the fear triggers presented to us.

The basic anatomy and physiology of the brain—and thus the way we initially react to danger—haven't changed much since the days of early humans. Our brains are hardwired to remain on constant alert for any potential threats that can cause bodily harm, which can lead to our fear-arousal system constantly being triggered by the experiences of modern daily life—that is, if we don't find ways to better navigate our initial reactions to triggers.

The basic anatomy and physiology of the brain—and thus the way we initially react to danger—haven't changed much since the days of early humans.

Thankfully, courage is in fact contagious.

When I reacted to the snake with courageous calm, it was easier for my students to also behave bravely. Was I startled? Hell yes, I was! But I had enough field experience not to overreact to animals in the wild. Because of my experience and neurohacks, I was able to use the gap between my initial emotional reaction and how I behaved to choose calm over panic. And the rattlesnake slithered merrily into the bushes with not a single student even shuffling their feet.

We will never remove our initial biological reactions to potential threats. But we can gain control over how we react to them, begetting even more bravery in ourselves and those around us.

Your Amygdala Keeps Score

Have you ever wondered why certain fears seem to stick with you no matter how much you try to shake them off? This tenacity of fear is largely due to the work of our danger alert system, the amygdala, aka "The Smoke Detector." This tiny but mighty warrior is a key player in the limbic system and is responsible for the processing of emotions, particularly fear.

Our amygdala also holds the power to imprint stressful experiences into our memory. It's like a vigilant sentinel, constantly on the lookout for potential threats so it can prepare us to survive. In doing so it helps us remember what's dangerous and, in turn, how to protect ourselves in the future.

The human brain constantly sifts through a huge amount of stimuli to determine what's most important to our goals and our survival. Sometimes a shortcut—a trigger—is needed to make processing all that data faster. And a trigger is simply that, a shortcut to faster information processing. We've become accustomed to thinking of triggers as negative, but a trigger is just something—a sound, smell, sight, or feeling—that elicits an emotional reaction because it's associated with a specific experience.

Most of us love eating cookies, and the smell of them baking might make you happy because it reminds you of your grandma's house. Conversely, the smell of cookies may make you nauseated because of the food poisoning you once got by ignoring the "do not eat raw" label on the ready-to-cook dough.

I shoulder scrunch and anxiously hold my breath whenever I can hear rainwater under speeding tires. While driving through pouring San Francisco rain, I totaled my beloved Mitsubishi Eclipse with the *Fast and Furious*–inspired rear spoiler (it was the early 2000s, don't judge). Even if I'm not the driver—the sound of tires trying to find purchase on a rain-slicked road sends all my fear bells ringing.

The amygdala learns how to keep us safe by maintaining a running scorecard of all the triggers we've associated with an experience, especially those that were very negative.

CHALLENGE OR THREAT?

It's impossible to showcase all your talent and truly meet your expectations when you feel under constant threat. This is because we're not biologically designed for it. When we experience a fear response, every aspect of our higher-level thinking slows down. Processing complicated situations, navigating emotions, even concentrating on everyday tasks, such as driving or making a cup of coffee, can become difficult, if not impossible. It simply takes too much brain power. Stress—which more accurately should be called a state of fear arousal—profoundly impacts all aspects of our lives.

Stress—which more accurately should be called a state of fear arousal—profoundly impacts all aspects of our lives.

While speaking at a conference in Switzerland on Neurohacking Courage, an attendee named Olya asked me why some stressful situations can be motivating while others are not. For example, an impending deadline can energize you to finish the project, or it can intimidate you so much that you miss the deadline altogether. Our response to stressful situations is part physical, part emotional, and part cognitive. But the difference

A QUICK REFRESH OF OUR FEAR/COURAGE CAST

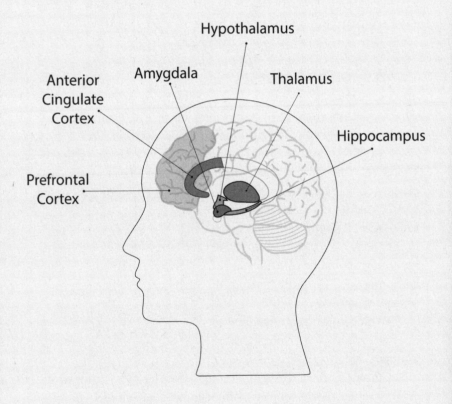

Just in case you need a quick refresher on these essential brain structures from our last chapter, here is a handy illustration:

BRAIN STRUCTURES IMPORTANT IN THE FEAR-AROUSAL RESPONSE	PRIMARY FUNCTION
Amygdala, "The Smoke Detector"	"The Smoke Detector," always on the lookout for threats. Regulates emotions and survival instincts.
Prefrontal Cortex (PFC), "The Command Center"	Responsible for higher cognitive functions: logic-based thought processing, emotional regulation, rational decision making, judgment, communication, goal setting, and the ability to understand ourselves and the world around us.
Hippocampus, "The Memory Maestro"	Processes long-term memory and regulates stress.
Thalamus, "The Relay Station"	Except for smell, all information from the body's senses is processed through the thalamus before being sent to the cerebral cortex for interpretation.
Hypothalamus, "The Thermostat"	Regulates body temperature, hunger, thirst, fatigue, sleep, and circadian rhythms.
Anterior Cingulate Cortex (ACC), "The Mediator"	Helps regulate emotions and resolve internal conflicts between what we think and what we feel.

between an energizing experience and an overwhelming one is our perception of the situation. Do we see it as a challenge or a threat? Challenges are situations where we feel we have the resources and skills to succeed. When we feel challenged, we can easily see the opportunities for growth and achievement. However, when we feel a situation is dangerous or that we don't have the resources or skills to be successful, that is when we move into a threat response.

Less than 24 hours after giving that talk, I'd walk this very tightrope between challenge and threat while ascending the Italian side of Mont Blanc, which is one of Europe's highest peaks at nearly 16,000 feet, in an incredibly safe rotating gondola. Soaring over ancient glaciers at vertigo-inducing heights, Craig and I quickly arrived at the highest summit access point, Station Punta Hellbronner. We were both safe, but I was the only one not okay. As Craig was frolicking around the empty gondola like Tigger on a sugar high, my breathing was shallow, my mouth dry, and, according to my iWatch heart monitor, the gondola was not the only thing soaring.

Even though my rational brain, mainly my prefrontal cortex, knew that I was perfectly safe (I mean, gondolas depart every 15 minutes on the Mont Blanc cableway), my fear arousal was still in overdrive as I switched my death grip from the gondola's internal railing to Craig's arm. I was, without a doubt, having an amygdala-driven fear response.

Even though I wouldn't describe myself as having a fear of heights—I mean, I did jump out of a perfectly good airplane and rappel thousands of feet down various waterfalls and canyons in Central America. But the fleeting miles of ground swooshing by while I was ensconced in a frequently used gondola was too much for my overtaxed amygdala, the pair of almond-shaped brain structures that drive our fear arousal responses.

As we emerged from the gondola at nearly the top of the mountain, we were greeted by the windy, snow-covered entry point plateau that served as the peak's base camp for ice hikers looking to ascend the remaining climb. My reaction? I was bear-hugging any solid railing I could find. The base camp plateau was perhaps 20 feet wide, with sheer cliff drops on each side. Perched in the middle was a gear hut and a tiny café that served both day trippers like Craig and me just up for a look around, but also the ice hikers and mountaineers about to risk their lives to experience life at the top of the world. There is very little room for error when mountaineering the highest peaks of the Alps, and in that moment, I felt like this relatively safe waystation was no different.

With shaky legs, I desperately held onto any railing I could find with one hand and Craig with the other as I stumbled into the café for a bit of a sit down away from the craggy sheer drops outside. After my initial waves of terror and nausea subsided, I began to think about not just my perceived threat response, but Olya's question in my workshop the previous day: What was the difference between challenge and threat?

I didn't necessarily feel unsafe in that moment. Logically, I knew I was not in danger. However, if a threat response is triggered when perceiving a lack of skills, resources, or support, then a challenge can quickly turn into threat. I had stepped onto the gondola without a hint of worry. I assumed, given my previous experiences, that it would be a fun, no-big-deal kind of ride. Unfortunately, I made this assumption based on my pre-pandemic self. It didn't cross my mind to make allowances for who I was at that moment, after so much time confined to my house instead of my normal state of global roaming.

Our amygdala is prone to being incredibly primitive and binary in how it helps us process our experiences—safe versus not safe, threat versus not a threat. Nuances and spectrums are the realm of our prefrontal cortex, which is the other major player in our biologically based fear responses. Our prefrontal cortex, or PFC, is where our logic and reason have their headquarters to help us make the best decisions and plan for the future. Unfortunately, when the amygdala is triggered and in fear-response mode, the PFC goes functionally offline, which is why we make such bad decisions when we're in a fear-arousal state.

As I watched thousands of feet whoosh by, my brain, which had gotten accustomed to only experiencing the world from my house or my very flat city in the previous two years, promptly lost its ever-loving wits. It didn't matter that I had done similar things before; my courage at that point had atrophied—something akin to an astronaut's muscles after being in space for mere days.

Perhaps you too are feeling like you "used to be" this or that. Or that the world seems scarier than it "used to be." It's important

Bravery Break: Connect 4

Ever play that game where you drop colored coins into a rack in the hopes of arranging four in a row before your competitor does? This neurohack is about connecting four of our senses to win back your calm from your amygdala, using your senses to make observations of your environment.

1. When you feel fear creeping in, pause and connect four observations using each of your senses: sight, sound, smell, and touch.

2. Out loud or to yourself, name a single something that you see four times, then repeat the same exercise for what you hear, smell, and touch, four times for each.

3. Repeat as needed.

For example, let's say I'm about to walk on stage to deliver an invited lecture. As my eyes roam over the multiple tiers of attendees in residence, my fear-arousal meter begins to climb. To bring a sense of calm back to my racing heart, I could begin by observing the red velvet stage curtain, repeating "red velvet curtain" to myself four times. Then, I would move on to the click-clacking of heels on the tiled floor, the smooth rubber of my mic cord, and the smell of hot electronics, repeating four times each.

to give yourself a lot of wiggle room because it both is and is not. If we're honest with each other, the world, in general, will never be easy or without threats. Your power is in your ability to change your perception from threats into challenges that you can then overcome and surpass. Mont Blanc's gondola ride reminded me that it's okay to white-knuckle the safety railing while others are literally frolicking around in the great expanse. Not everyone's stories are the same, but that doesn't mean we're not all equally courageous.

Merely showing up is brave, no matter what that looks like. For me, crawling out of the gondola and holding onto anything stable didn't mean I was a coward; I was a human attempting to make brave choices even when my world felt like it was tilting sideways.

THE AMYGDALA IN ACTION

When a fear stressor is detected, your body instinctively responds with a reaction of fight, flight, freeze, or fawn. These primal reactions, deeply rooted in our evolutionary history, are part of a broader collection of sympathetic nervous system responses that prepare us to deal with potentially dangerous events. Remember, the sympathetic and parasympathetic nervous systems —the "gas pedal" and the "brakes," respectively—are the two subdivisions of our autonomic nervous system responsible for keeping our body functioning that we covered in Chapter 4.

Fight-or-flight response

Picture this: You're driving down the road when suddenly a child darts in front of your car in pursuit of a red rubber ball. In that moment your brain springs into action, and your fear responses activate. Your eyes and ears relay vital information about what's happening to your amygdala. As your brain's emotion-processing powerhouse, it swiftly decodes the images and sounds received and decides between danger or safety. As your car careens toward the oblivious child, your amygdala chooses danger and immediately sends a distress signal to another part of your brain, the hypothalamus.

The hypothalamus, your body's command center for survival, serves as a liaison between your brain and the rest of your body. Once it gets this distress call from the amygdala, it triggers the release of epinephrine (aka adrenaline) and initiates a series of physiological changes to increase heart rate, blood flow, and breathing to deliver extra oxygen throughout the body, making you feel more alert, energized, and focused.

This exchange between the amygdala and hypothalamus is so incredibly fast that it starts to happen before the visual center of your brain has even had a chance to fully process the scene. This priority of action over awareness is why this process is often called "instinctual," which is why some people say, "I don't know what happened; I just reacted."

In this scenario (hopefully!), you would take action toward the perceived stressor (fight) by slamming on the brakes in lieu of opening the car door, barrel-rolling out, and running in the opposite direction (flight).

Freeze

Freezing is a reaction to a stressful event where, well, you can't move or react to a distressing trigger. There are two types of freeze responses: The first is where your body freezes in order to gather enough information on the situation to react, and the second involves a prolonged freeze where you can't react because your brain decides that neither fighting nor fleeing is the best path to survival.

An example of an instant freeze would be when you're woken from a deep sleep by a loud noise. You then stay perfectly still, holding your breath, waiting for more sensory information to determine if someone is breaking into your home or it's just your home making one of its settling sounds.

An example of a more prolonged freeze happens in just about every horror film. It's the moment where the audience is practically screaming "Run! Run!" while the camera zooms in on a terrified teen with a face drained of color who can't seem to do anything but pant and stare wide-eyed in the presence of danger.

Flinch

Flinching is a product of your startle response, an automatic reaction of muscle contraction that allows you to jump or arc away from a potential threat. Flinching is usually short-lived and doesn't have any intense lingering effects. Unlike the other four responses to fear, when you flinch your body processes the threat quickly and then may move into another fear response, like fleeing or fighting, based on how the situation progresses.

Something to consider: If you think you're prone to startling more easily than others, you might be living in a heightened state of fear. Recent research has revealed that people with a strong startle reflex are more likely to be struggling with anxiety or trauma. Like a light switch stuck in the on position, their bodies may be continually operating in a state of heightened fear arousal, or hypervigilance, as their sympathetic nervous system spends more time in charge than their rest-and-digest parasympathetic nervous system.

Fawn

Fawning is when the body reacts with submissive or pleasing behavior toward an aggressor in order to escape danger. A fawning reaction to a threat is when the brain decides, based on previous experience, that neither fighting nor fleeing will result in safety. Fawning is localized to dangerous situations with stressors that can be reasoned with. For example, a child being bullied by an aggressive classmate may compliment the bully or promise favors in order to escape a beating. They may duck their head low and try to appear small and nonthreatening.

This type of reaction to a threat is most common in those who have been abused. Someone trying to use fawning to avoid danger will be overly agreeable and super helpful to an aggressor in an attempt to please their way out of pain and suffering. Even after the abuser is removed, fawning can become a go-to survival mechanism for those who have experienced trauma, creating patterns of constant people-pleasing as their brains attempt to keep their bodies safe. Those who have become reliant on fawning as a survival mechanism often lack personal boundaries, rely too heavily on others' opinions, and many times can be easily manipulated.

FROM FAWNER TO FIGHTER

Although my transition from people-pleasing fawn to power fighter didn't happen overnight—and frankly is a lifelong journey—I can claim this one memorable milestone.

Being raised in fear meant that my go-to survival strategies were to run and hide or fawn. Once in the professional world, the whole run-and-hide-in-the-bathroom tactic didn't work well, so I relied heavily on fawning techniques of acquiescing and placating, no matter the personal cost to me.

While putting myself through grad school, I worked in corporate accounts payable in downtown Oakland, California. My slate-blue fabric cubicle had a two-by-two-foot window that overlooked a brick building six inches away. It was a train-as-you go position since the only previous finance experience I had was being robbed at gunpoint at the tender age of eighteen while working as an entry-level bank teller.

After a few years of going above and beyond what was asked of me, including never saying no, I knew in my heart that it wasn't the place for me. On the outside it was a great position, especially while I was finishing my research degree: full-time, benefits, security. An absolute dream job for some—but it wasn't *my* dream job. Then I graduated with my first master's degree in biology, and still I stayed. Because it was safe. Because it was easier to suffer through the daily drudgery of doing something I hated instead of jumping into the unknown.

My daily house-to-car-to-park-to-BART-train-to-walk-from-the-station-to-the-office commute was an hour each way. Back and forth. Day in and day out. After graduation, when I didn't leave, something shifted in how management saw me. I had always been the "yes girl," but my staying put (which in my mind was safe) somehow gave them what they needed to turn up the heat on how much "value" they could get out of my time. Like the proverbial frog in boiling water, the heat kept going higher and higher, but still I stayed. I didn't balk because I was the good girl, the team player, the fawn.

Then one day, I couldn't sit down without shooting pain in my tailbone.

I hadn't fallen or been in an accident. I hadn't gone snowboarding or really done anything other than sit on my backside for sixty hours a week, entering invoices into QuickBooks and dodging calls from vendors asking why we hadn't paid them yet (I learned to send everything to voicemail way before it was cool).

Six months and twice as many doctors later, I came to the realization that my job had literally become a pain in my ass.

From X-rays to MRIs, GPs to acupuncture, I was told over and over again that nothing was wrong. And yet nothing worked to stop the intense shooting pain. I was at a loss for what to do next and scared that this was my new life now, so I did what I always did—I hid from reality and tried to fawn my way out by taking on more work, being even nicer to senior leadership, and generally trying to be the best little doormat that company had ever seen!

All of which, as usual, did nothing helpful.

The turning point happened in an innocuous beer garden in downtown San Jose. I was meeting with my former major professor, Dr. John Matson, to catch up on life post-grad. With his signature long gray ponytail dripping down the back of his trademark Jack Hannah safari shirt with enough pockets to make a backpack inconsequential, he asked, "So, what exactly are you doing with your life?"

Wow, John. I haven't even had my first glass of chardonnay yet. Damn.

But of course he was right. After I told him my tale of woe, his advice was spot-on. I didn't spend years and thousands and thousands of dollars to be an accounts payable assistant. But the rub was that I wasn't just covering *my* living costs; I was also providing for Momma Helen as well. It felt like enough to justify staying in a job I hated, one that was suffocating me and that was literally a huge pain in my ass.

COURAGE QUEST:
Rebuilding from the Wreckage

A popular metaphor for personal transformation is the butterfly, and you probably recall from your K–12 days the simple diagram showing its unique process of metamorphosis. In three simple images, the caterpillar becomes a chrysalis and finally bursts into a majestic adult butterfly. But the reality is far more messy and more akin to the actual process of personal transformation than we may initially think. Once inside the chrysalis, change is slow and gradual as the caterpillar's body digests itself from the inside out.

The raw materials of transforming into the new must come from dissolving the old. For the new to be built, the old must be broken down so it can be used for parts.

In this Courage Quest, think back to a transformational time in your life. It could be marked by a milestone: graduation, birth, divorce, death. Or it could just be a season of emotional or spiritual transformation. Then:

- Describe this time in your life. Try to bring in as many sensory memories as possible. What was the weather like? Who else was there? Can you recall a song you would play on repeat?

- Can you articulate or describe what fears were swirling around your head during this time?

- Can you recall a moment during that season of change when you felt like a dissolved pile of goo? That in-between phase where you were no longer who you were, nor were you who you would become?

- What gave you the courage to rebuild from the wreckage?

I must have looked pretty dejected because Dr. Matson extended a much-needed rescue branch. "Look, why don't you come teach a single class for me? It won't be the same money as your full-time gig, but it will be science, and it will be changing lives, the two reasons you went to school in the first place."

So I did.

That one conversation with a valued mentor gave me the strength and confidence to push back and stand up for the hopes and dreams I had set for myself, versus just going along with what others, namely my managers and my mother, wanted from me. It gave me the courage to jump into the unknown. Sometimes change happens in tiny steps, and sometimes it happens by way of a massive leap across the great divide.

The next day, I quit my accounts payable job, took that single teaching class for the term, went back to waiting tables to cover the difference, and never looked back.

And the big surprise?

My tailbone pain vanished the day after I quit. Poof. Gone.

It wasn't magic. It was me addressing a psychosomatic manifestation of my dread that I would never live up to my potential, along with my growing panic about living a life unlived and dying at my little desk overlooking that brick wall. Once I stepped into a space of courage to stand up for what I wanted in my life and welcomed an unknown future, the pain in my bum was gone.

It's been more than twenty years since that day when I chose to bravely step into the void over the perceived safety of hiding and fawning away my life. Like yours, my life has been a constant roller coaster of peaks and valleys, but I can say that my dedication to choosing science and changing lives has never faltered since.

And my phantom tailbone pain was never felt again.

ARE YOU AMYGDALA OR PREFRONTAL CORTEX DRIVEN?

As a lifelong comic book nerd and lover of sci-fi and fantasy, I'm forever attracted to the pairing of characters that represent emotion versus logic—which is not unlike the amygdala and the prefrontal cortex, the two main characters in the story of fear and courage.

The amygdala's main character trait would be action, while the prefrontal cortex (PFC) would be common sense and logic.

From the Marvel cinematic universe, we have Chris Hemsworth's thunder god Thor, who is like your amygdala—all about action, moving, fighting, protecting. He runs toward the danger, even if he doesn't have a plan. He's the character with big muscles and a heart of gold who always has the best intentions but isn't exactly the brightest crayon in the box. The trickster god Loki, played by Tom Hiddleston, would be your PFC. Loki is always plotting and planning, trying to think his way out of trouble (that he generally got himself into in the first place). Similarly, your PFC is trying to help you stay ten steps ahead of everyone else, using as much information as possible to help you avoid danger using logic and superior intellect.

A more retro example would be Kirk and Spock from *Star Trek*. Kirk was, of course, the official captain, always making decisions with his heart and not his head. He would sometimes need Spock, who was forever data-driven and analytical, to take over if he was running around on a dangerous planet, being his emotionally rash self. Sort of the perfect example of the interplay between our PFC and amygdala—because there can only be one captain of the ship at a time.

When your amygdala is triggered, your logic-based prefrontal cortex basically takes a little nap, causing you to make poor decisions and stifling your creativity. By recognizing your fear response in the moment and applying strategies to put your prefrontal cortex back in the captain's chair, you can regain your clarity of thought and control to make the best choices possible and move forward.

So, which one is the captain of your decisions: logic or emotion, your PFC or your amygdala?

These ideas go back as far as Aristotle's teachings on persuasion, where a communicator should balance their appeal to logic (Logos) with their appeal to the audience's emotions (Pathos). Ignoring either one can lead to less-than-ideal outcomes. But here's what science tells us about how often we tend to go one way or the other. In a recent study combining engagement data with fMRI (functional magnetic resonance imaging), Gallup found that 70 percent of decisions we make are emotionally driven, with only a paltry 30 percent based on logic-driven rational factors.

Whether it's through stories like Logos/Pathos or characters such as Spock and Kirk or Loki and Thor, the importance of trying to balance our internal logic and emotions is a big part of survival and managing our fears.

Mirror Neurons: Why Courage and Fear Are Contagious

Mirror neurons are so named because they mirror the emotions of those around you. These specialized brain cells are activated when we witness another person performing an action or expressing an emotion. Mirror neurons are designed to help us understand, empathize, and respond to the behaviors, intentions, and emotional states of others. When our mirror neurons fire, it allows us to recognize the emotional experience in another and maybe even experience it ourselves (a phenomenon called "emotional contagion").

The concept of mirror neurons explains why we can feel emotions such as joy or sadness just by seeing them expressed by someone else, either in person or via media.

The concept of mirror neurons explains why we can feel emotions such as joy or sadness just by seeing them expressed by someone else, either in person or via media. The same goes for anger, disgust, and any of our other core emotions. This is partly why you are what you eat when it comes to the media you consume. Munch on nothing but angry pundits screaming the news out? Your mirror neurons will help you feel angrier even if you don't really have anything in your own life to be angry about. Conversely, slurping up regular daily bowls of positive content that reinforces the values most important to you will help increase your happiness, empathy, and yes, courage.

Additionally, your own emotional state can directly impact other people, whose mirror neurons also allow them to get a sense of your mental state.

HOW MIRROR NEURONS KEEP US SAFE

Have you ever felt that something was dangerous, but couldn't say why?

Most of us have instinctively avoided a public interaction without being able to articulate the reason, guided by our brain's protective instincts. Our brain constantly gathers information subconsciously, which can trigger a fear response without us knowing exactly why. This is thanks, in part, to mirror neurons which help us understand others' intentions and warn us when something seems off, making us feel distrustful or uncomfortable. Conversely, when those around us are calm, it helps us feel safe, even in potentially dangerous situations.

Seeing the Bars, So You Can Find the Door

Courage isn't just about grand heroic acts—it's also about the small, everyday actions we take to connect with others, to empathize, to understand. Only when we can clearly see the biological cages we were all born into, can we begin to find the door.

Recognizing our biological constraints fosters empathy and a deeper understanding that our responses to life are not always within our control, and that's perfectly okay. It's just part of being human. But we're also not creatures at the mercy of our amygdala. Yes, they can be a right proper pain when they're overreacting, but with the knowledge you're gaining here, you can find ways to strengthen your courage muscles through practice and neurohacks.

It's only when we start to see the bars of our cages that we can start to break free, which inspires others to do the same.

When you change, so does the world.

CHAPTER 6

Societal Fear: Why Others Make Us Afraid

I cannot escape death—but at least I can escape the fear of it.
—EPICTETUS

Language, the principal form of how we communicate, is how the customs, beliefs, and values of any society are passed among members and across generations. From stories to songs, language is how we learn, share, and grow. It is also how we spread fear.

Whether written, spoken, or gestured, how we communicate fear has a profound impact on us all. Fearmongering, a persuasion tactic, communicates exaggerated or false information in order to instill fear as a way to control, manipulate, and exploit others. Left unchecked, it can lead a society to become more violent, aggressive, intolerant, and discriminatory. Constant gloom-and-doom communications can also cause people to withdraw from society, becoming isolated, depressed, and lonely. It can also lead to a lack of trust in institutions and even other people, eroding the fabric of any society.

Language has power.

Words like "terrorist" have been used to justify wars, surveillance, and laws that limit rights and freedoms. Fearmongering rhetoric is used even more during times of crisis or uncertainty, when people are more likely to be swayed by powerful emotions such as fear and anger.

I was a college freshman when the 9/11 terrorist attack occurred. This was before the internet was an all-encompassing thing, and I remember being glued to the TV and radio, along with the rest of the nation, for any and all news. In the days and weeks that followed, some of my most vivid memories are of media outlets hyper-focusing on the violence. Their coverage made it

---

A Note on Context

When I use the term "Western society" or just "society," I'm referring to the many groups of people who share a broad set of customs, beliefs, social norms, ethical values, political systems, and practices that evolved from ancient Greece. Most people would include the modern regions of the Americas, United Kingdom, and European Union as Western societies. I want to acknowledge that the Western view is not absolute truth. But having spent my life living primarily in the United States and England, with some time in Australia, it's where my familiarity lives, as those societies influenced most of my personal experiences shared in this book.

I would never attempt to speak for cultures that I do not have a deep understanding of or experience with, so if you find that my take on fear in society doesn't resonate with your particular cultural experience, I encourage you to contact me through MaryPoffenroth.com. I would love to hear how your cultural experience with fear and courage differed from mine, and hey, who knows, maybe the next book will be *Brave New You: Global Edition*! That would be a dream come true!

---

seem like terrorism was now an ever-present threat to our country, something that we needed to be constantly vigilant about. This "us-versus-them" narrative implied that we should be wary of our neighbors or "we could be next," resulting in violent acts committed in the name of staying "safe."

Of course we all want to feel safe. We want to trust our leaders and their decisions. We want to believe what we read, hear, and see. But when fearmongering, or stoking fear, becomes a primary way of communicating, it can have an incredibly damaging effect on society if left unchecked.

Fearonomics: The Selling and Marketing of Fear

Why are we constantly subjected to a never-ending barrage of propaganda designed to keep us in a constant state of fear?

Scared people spend money to feel safe.

The economy of fear thrives on the idea that we are always in danger and that the only way to protect ourselves is to purchase products that promise us security and help us mitigate risk. By highlighting worst-case scenarios, advertisers commonly use dread over being unlovable, or worry about being safe, or trepidation around health to promote a product or service.

The economy of fear thrives on the idea that we are always in danger and that the only way to protect ourselves is to purchase products that promise us security and help us mitigate risk.

Scared people make poor decisions.

By playing on our anxieties and insecurities, we're encouraged to consume products that promise us love, protection, and security, even if the threat is not necessarily real. We're constantly consuming messages that fill us with the fear of missing out (FOMO), make us anxious about our job security, and play on our worries about the future of our planet.

Scared people are easier to control.

Advertisers understand that our brains are wired to respond to threats, making it a highly effective form of manipulation. By tapping into our innate desire for self-preservation, along with our natural inclination to fear the unknown, we're more likely to listen if the message is framed as a warning against something danger-ous or damaging—regardless if it's actually true. In response, we immediately feel the urge to protect ourselves and those we love, so we do things like buying a security alarm to give us the illusion of safety.

Which is why it's vital to become more aware of the impact that fear-based communication has on our daily life, so you can seek to shatter the illusion of constant danger.

SELLING LOVE TO "THE UNLOVABLE"

Just as preying on our fears around personal safety is big business, targeting our suspicions that we are "unlovable" is another reliable way to get us to buy things.

Here's how it works: If you think you're somehow unlovable, you will be more vulnerable to marketing that promises to magically transform your life from drab to dazzling in Cinderella-like fashion. But these ads are rarely what they seem. First off, you're lovable as you are right now. Second, if an ad is promising to fix your deeply emotional thoughts or perceptions with a quick wave of a mascara wand, run the other way. The only thing they're selling is a big lie. For advertisers, capitalizing on the dreams and nightmares of a tar-get demographic is Marketing 101.

And one of the worst offenders today in this regard is the beauty industry.

Don't get me wrong, I love the artistry of makeup, am very into skincare, and am a card-carrying Rouge-level VIP at Sephora. However, the way that many beauty products are advertised is frankly vile. Take, for example, the skin-lightening ad I came across while in an airport in Thailand. It showed a woman with darker skin looking dejected and sad. Her boyfriend had broken up with her to be with a woman who had lighter skin. So, rather than purging the colorist dirtbag from her heart, she buys the advertised product and bleaches her skin from head to toe. Then, when her old boyfriend sees her, he immediately wants her back. And she takes him back! And she's . . . happy? I almost burst into tears right there in Terminal 1.

Fear-based marketing is an insidious and toxic type of advertising that plays on our insecurities and vulnerabilities to manipulate us into buying something. But we can fight back and avoid being taken advantage of by this type of marketing. The first step is knowing what it looks like.

Fear-based ads often use language that triggers anxiety or worry, while making exaggerated claims about potential dangers or risks associated with *not* buying the product or service. These ad campaigns sometimes also use scarcity tactics, such as "limited time" offers or discounts that make you feel like you need to act quickly before an opportunity passes you by.

Fear-based marketing is an insidious and toxic type of advertising that plays on our insecurities and vulnerabilities to manipulate us into buying something.

The great thing is that, once you start to look for them, you can't unsee these tactics. They become so glaringly blatant that it's easy for you to steer clear of any company trying to use emotional manipulation to increase profits. Lodge your disgust for fearmongering by voting with your dollars and only purchasing from companies that align with your values.

Companies change when consumers change.

COURAGE QUEST: Who Are You in Society?

We're all products of our environment. Our beliefs, behaviors, and the personas we adopt are shaped by the world around us. This includes our sociopolitical identities, which can potentially influence our capacity for courage.

Sociopolitical identities exist at the intersection of your social and political self. They're who you are in the context of society. For example, one of my sociopolitical identities is that I'm a woman with a PhD in a male-dominated industry, which motivates me to deeply care about the education and empowerment of women.

Our sociopolitical identities consist of our political affiliations, religious beliefs, and social associations. These identities resonate with our core values and offer a sense of belonging. But they can also be a source of fear and anxiety. Fear of exclusion, fear of judgment, fear of being different—these are anxieties deeply rooted in our sociopolitical identities.

Sociopolitical identities can act as an invisible boundary, confining us to a comfort zone. The fear of crossing these boundaries can inhibit our courage to explore, question, and grow. They are complex, nuanced constructs that shape our worldviews and influence our actions. They can also influence what we're afraid of and what gives us the strength to keep moving forward, no matter the cost.

Since our sociopolitical identities can both empower and constrain us, it's important to know which ones are most important to us. Dive deeper into your own sociopolitical identity by choosing from the following list three identities that are so important to you that you would march, rally, donate, and fight on their behalf. Once you have your top three, detail how you specifically show up for them. Do your routine choices and actions reinforce their importance to others? If not, why?

Age/generational groupings	Occupation/employment status
Body type/size	Parental status
Education level	Physical ability/disabilities
Gender identity	Political affiliation
Immigration status	Race/ethnicity
Language proficiency	Religious beliefs
Marital status	Sexual orientation
Mental health conditions	Socioeconomic status
National origin	Veteran status
Neighborhood/geographic location	

Fear in Modern Media

Media in all forms is one of the primary methods of communicating fear within society. Media disseminators big and small commonly use foreboding and dread to increase ratings or bolster audience engagement. When you factor in that anyone with basic technology (who lives in a somewhat democratic country) can become their own media maker, it means there are even more opportunities for unsubstantiated rumors and deliberate misinformation to spread. And this kind of "information" can create a sense of panic, especially when it is false or exaggerated. When we only consume stories of violence and tragedy we feel more anxious, overwhelmed, and afraid.

TRAINING OUR BRAINS FOR TRAGEDY

When we see or hear fear-inducing stories, it causes us to mentally rehearse doom-and-gloom scenarios. This activates a fear response in our prefrontal cortex without us being in immediate danger. And, of course, social media can make fear-driven shame and stress worse. Constant connectivity, the relentless nature of the online news cycle, and the increased scrutiny of living our lives before an unseen audience mean that our fear response is continually triggered. And because of the ever-expanding nature of our online lives, from the deluge of images to personal brands, the feeling of being under "threat" never ends.

Modern life allows for an unprecedented amount of time and mind space for higher-level concerns like social interaction, status anxiety, and personal fulfillment. And the more time we spend comparing ourselves to others and obsessing over our self-image, online or otherwise, the more time our brains spend negotiating the "threat" of being shunned for a silly (but impossible-to-delete) mistake.

But the sense of danger we experience via our screens, our tendency to "compare and despair" on social media, is just the beginning. In addition to a heightened state of fear arousal, prolonged exposure to violent content can have long-term neurological implications. In extreme cases, it can even lead to post-traumatic stress disorder (PTSD). This means that people who merely watched videos of violent events, without witnessing them in person, struggled with similar symptoms as those who actually experienced traumatic events.

Research has shown that people exposed to violent incidents (either in person or through digital media) reported feeling "dehumanized" and "desensitized" when they viewed similar events. This could potentially lead them to develop an intense fear of a similar situation happening in their own lives, reducing empathy for victims of violence or leading them to believe that extreme violence is a normal part of life.

LIVING IN THE AGE OF INFORMATION OVERLOAD
It's no surprise that our brains feel overwhelmed and stressed. Most of us are constantly bombarded by emails, social media, news

updates, and message pings on our phones, laptops, and tablets. It can feel relentless, a phenomenon commonly referred to as cognitive overload.

The amount of information the human brain can process at one time is limited, and cognitive overload occurs when we exceed that capacity. When we hit our limit, our ability to focus becomes impaired, robbing us of the ability to make good decisions or retain new information (hello, brain fog, I see you!).

The amount of information the human brain can process at one time is limited, and cognitive overload occurs when we exceed that capacity.

The capacity for new information is not fixed, but rather fluctuates based on the person or the type of information being processed. When the amount of incoming information surpasses the resources of an individual, like when we're trying to multitask our way out of a looming deadline, cognitive overload occurs. It can result in increased activation of fear responses, psychological distress, and feeling overwhelmed, anxious, and unable to cope with life's everyday demands.

Cognitive overload can also make us more vulnerable to falling into faulty reasoning and impaired decision-making traps. When overloaded, we're more likely to accept information that is incorrect, biased, or agenda-driven without considering the reliability of the source or alternative data. In this state, we're more susceptible to misinformation and unrealistic evaluations of actual risk, which can lead to even greater anxiety.

CLICK HERE IF YOU WANT TO LIVE

Journalists and editors who are often under immense pressure to increase audience engagement sometimes resort to sensational content to create a false sense of danger, which entices people to click on the article (aka clickbait). Whether it's exaggerating facts or using language that creates an atmosphere of panic, creating content to scare someone into clicking on it causes people to be more fearful than they need to be.

This tactic is especially prevalent in health-related articles that feature warnings about the dangers of a given lifestyle choice or condition. This kind of fear stoking is effective at capturing attention and creating urgency, but it can also result in unnecessary panic while also building an atmosphere of mistrust between consumers and media outlets.

When people become too reliant on sensationalized news reports, their view of reality becomes skewed and they may start believing false information or conspiracy theories, with possibly serious consequences. When people become overly fearful because of exaggerated media reporting, they may take extreme measures such as stockpiling baby formula or carrying out a mass shooting at a place of worship—something that could otherwise be avoided if more accurate information was presented. Also, when constantly bombarded with negativity, people become desensitized and are less likely to take action when needed.

When overloaded, we're more likely to accept information that is incorrect, biased, or agenda-driven without considering the reliability of the source or alternative data.

Fear-based journalism in just about any form polarizes society by creating an "us-versus-them" mentality, one that eschews nuance or alternative perspectives and simply portrays one side as good and the other as evil. Instead of presenting facts and working hard to get all sides of a story, fear-driven reporting is one-sided and only serves to divide people further.

Bravery Break: The Near and Far of It

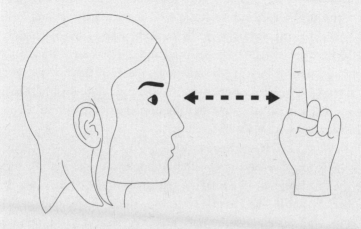

An easy, transportable way to bring calm to an excited amygdala is through a practice called convergent and divergent strategic eye movements. It sounds complex, but it is quite simple. Convergent eye movements happen when you cross your eyes, while divergent eye movements occur when you look outward, expanding your field of vision.

This neurohack will activate your vagus nerve, a key player in your body's stress response system. By doing this movement a few times when you are in the throes of a fear-arousal response, you can signal to your body that all is well, that you are safe.

Here's how to do it: Take a pen and hold it in front of your eyes resting against the tip of your nose. Then focus your eyes on it, which will result in your vision of the pen going blurry and in doubles. Now slowly move the pen away from your nose while still keeping your gaze focused on it until it is at the farthest point of your outstretched arm. Next, slowly bring it back to your nose while never losing focus on the pen. Repeat this a few times until you start to feel relief.

No pen, no problem! You can always just use your finger!

Doom Scrolling

Early internet creators dreamed of a digital utopia born from the magic of connecting people around the globe in seconds. They pictured an informed, healthier world with more education and love. And sure, in many ways, the existence of the web seems like magic! But the internet is equal parts sparkles and sadness. Instead of stoking intellectual or logical conversations, much of the internet and social media have become engines driven by emotion. Evoking emotion in media is nothing new, but the immense detrimental effects on mental and physical well-being are.

Pull down. Refresh. Repeat.

Being social creatures has allowed humans to successfully survive the hardships of life. Sharing resources and finding safety in numbers meant it was evolutionarily advantageous for our species to care about acceptance by individuals or within a community. However, we didn't evolve the capacity to consider, relate to, and internalize the opinions, emotions, and reactions of hundreds, let alone millions of people.

Living in pre-internet communities never demanded the kind of threat analysis that maintaining a "perfect" public persona entails today. As a result, our antiquated fear response runs rampant as we contemplate whether we should have posted that picture, while we compare and despair ourselves into deeper and deeper pits of anxiety.

Living in pre-internet communities never demanded the kind of threat analysis that maintaining a "perfect" public persona entails today.

During the early months of the pandemic, stuck at home with no way to take action or interact with the outside world beyond obsessively reading the news on my phone, I spent hours every day scrolling, commenting, liking, and sharing messages that aligned with my opinions, then scrolling some more. With each new post, I went from fired up to enraged to excited to devastated, all within minutes.

I craved community and connection, but with Los Angeles in citywide lockdown, I could only find it online. The logical part of my brain knew that constantly scrolling to relieve my anxiety over the unknown and scary (aka doom scrolling) was making my life worse, not better. But my emotional brain could not close the app. Doom scrolling was an escape from the helplessness I felt. If the world was burning down around me, I figured at least I'd be ready.

Pull down. Refresh. Repeat.

Deep within my fears of the unknown and the uncontrollable, I didn't feel concerned about my heavy news consumption because I justified those endless hours as "doing my research" and "being a good, well-informed citizen." I thought if I just consumed enough information, if I absorbed enough content, if I read enough pundit hot takes, I could get a handle on the situation. I could regain my lost sense of control. I could feel safe again.

But that's not what happened. My prefrontal cortex, which is all about anticipation, preparing, and planning, fired up my amygdala by mentally anticipating fear-inducing experiences as I was forever sending my brain to tragedy boot camp.

Wired for Connection

From the moment we're born, society quietly whispers in our ears, telling us what to fear and what not to fear. This subtle, continuous background track lives rent-free in our heads, and we grow so accustomed to it that we often don't even notice it until we really start to listen. When we dive deeper, we find a whole lot of our fears are just a reflection of societal norms passed onto us.

They are not really us.

Part of the challenge in parsing the signal from the noise is that our brains are wired to fit in. As a social species, the human amygdala sees community as safety and survival. In fact, numerous studies have shown that social support is absolutely essential for physical and psychological health. And this includes everything from stress resilience to trauma-related mental disorders to the survival and recovery rates of medical patients.

But being in society is hard. We're constantly surrounded by traditional markers of success, along with constant reminders of the stakes. The psychological burden of not meeting expectations of marriage, children, home ownership (or just being able to live without roommates from Craigslist), and financial security can be so incredibly heavy that we may withdraw from society out of fear, shame, and guilt. It can lead to feelings that other people just can't possibly relate to our difficulties (though I have a secret: everyone absolutely can!).

Another common worry revolves around being seen as difficult or unlovable, which causes us to fret over being judged. We can be so afraid of rejection that we mold ourselves into who we think society will accept because we're all terrified of dying alone. Society can be an ever-present specter, but we get to choose whether or not to listen to its haunting chants of "you aren't good enough" and "you have no control."

Humans created the society we were born into, so we, as humans, absolutely have the power to reshape that society into one of authenticity, transparency, respect, and tolerance.

Societal cages can feel too vast to be changed, but I would disagree. Humans created the society we were born into, so we, as humans, absolutely have the power to reshape that society into one of authenticity, transparency, respect, and tolerance. A place where our communications serve to inspire, innovate, and include.

So how do we break free from the societal chains of expectation while at the same time reaping the benefits of community and connection? By being hyper-aware of the exact societal pressures that contribute to our stress. A degree of insecurity is a natural part of life, but once we have the tools to better navigate the discomfort that insecurity brings, we can more easily reject persuasive communications that don't align with our core values.

We can start to smash the locks by using our knowledge to take actionable steps, such as actively decreasing our exposure to communications that are only meant to incite fear or manipulate. We can then begin to free others by harnessing and sharing the wisdom we've gained. When we start to spread our shared beliefs, practices, and values through education and transparency—instead of fear, guilt, and shame—we begin to build a more inclusive and courageous tomorrow.

CHAPTER 7

Personal Fear: When We Make Ourselves Afraid

It's not the load that breaks you down;
it's the way you carry it.
—LENA HORNE

M y biological father was Indigenous American, while my biological mother was of European descent. As a young girl, I
remember repeatedly being told that I was lucky to have been born
presenting white. My Apache-Comanche Auntie Myrtle, who helped
raise me alongside Momma Helen, stressed how important it was to
"protect my whiteness," since, like many mixed heritage humans,
my skin could easily become dramatically darker with even a single
day of unprotected sunshine due to the ease with which my body
produces melanin. I was taught early on that to live in the United
States was to understand that skin color equated to safe versus not
safe. My brain was trained to be afraid of tanning.

One incredibly vivid memory from childhood is of riding horseback with Auntie Myrtle through the tall summer grass. Squinting to convey her earnestness, she turned to me and said, "Looking white keeps you safe." Auntie Myrtle was raised on "The Rez" and had experienced all the struggles of a lifetime presenting non-white, no matter how much sun she got.

I dreamed of being accepted by society and living safe from violence, so I internalized this message so deeply that I have devoted untold hours of my life and who knows how much money to sun protection. Even though I don't get sunburns, my bathroom drawer is filled with fifteen different kinds of sunscreen, while my closet is filled with big floppy hats, massive sunglasses, and SPF sun shirts. In fact, I purchased five of the same black floppy hat to store in various locations, from my car to backpacks, just in case I leave the house without one. I internalized the message that protecting my skin from the sun meant I was protecting myself from racism and ill treatment. Of course, as with many of the fears unique to each of us, I didn't really give this obsessive sun protection behavior any deeper thought. It was just how things were done.

What habits might you have that have a deeper root in fear?

It's a Trap!

Do you ever find yourself stuck in a loop of negative thoughts? Or feel like an impostor despite your impressive accomplishments and achievements? Or berate yourself over who you "should" be?

Our amygdalas yearn to feel safe and in control, But we have so many mind traps to hide in as we struggle to manage the hardest parts of our lives. Mind traps are thoughts, beliefs, or self-talk that lead to limiting behavior. They consist of distorted views of reality and irrational ways of thinking that cause us to feel overwhelmed or inadequate. Common examples include thoughts around "I'm not good enough" or "I can never do anything right." These mental scripts are often based on past experiences and heavily influence our present-day decisions and behavior.

COMMON MIND TRAPS

MIND TRAP	DESCRIPTION	EXAMPLE
All-or-Nothing Thinking	Viewing a situation in binary terms instead of on a nuanced continuum.	Thinking you're an awful cook after failing the first and only time you tried.
Always Taking the Blame	Unfairly blaming oneself for events outside their control.	Apologizing because it rained during your family picnic.
Automatic Thoughts	Thoughts or images that are instantaneous responses to triggers.	Immediately responding to any criticism with "I'm worthless," "I'm a failure," "I'm no good," or "No one understands me."
Blaming Others	Holding anyone but yourself accountable when things go wrong.	"We didn't make our quarterly numbers because everyone on my team is lazy and incompetent."
Catastrophizing	Believing the worst possible scenario will come true or making negative interpretations without evidence to support your conclusion.	If we don't arrive on time for dinner, your mother will hate me and we'll need to call off the wedding.

Mind traps (aka cognitive distortions) come in many forms, but some common types include the following:

MIND TRAP	DESCRIPTION	EXAMPLE
Fortune Telling	Making bold, unsupported predictions or assuming others' thoughts and feelings without verification.	"I know he'll say no, so I'm not even going to ask."
Magnification and Minimization	Zooming in and exaggerating negatives (such as fears, disappointments, or losses) and minimizing or ignoring positives.	"I can't believe I cc'd the entire department. I'm so terrible at my job; I'm going to get fired."
Overgeneralization	Defining something or someone entirely by a rare negative event, assuming it's an unending pattern, or using absolutes like "all," "always," "never," or "none."	"Every person I date is always an immature loser. I'm never going to find love."
Should Statements	The tendency to impose a set of unrealistic or rigid rules or standards of behavior for yourself or others. Using words like "should" or "must."	"I must never cry in front of others because a successful woman should be seen as strong."

A theory first proposed by psychiatrist and researcher Aaron Beck, then popularized a decade later by his student David Burns, held that cognitive distortions are mind traps that we can fall into and then become stuck in. They can become patterns of unhelpful thinking and unhealthy behaviors, often leading to self-defeating thoughts and feelings that limit our potential and make it difficult to move forward in life, leaving us feeling insecure and frustrated.

These mind traps, or cognitive distortions, are believed to come from cognitive bias, a phenomenon rooted in our brain's attempt to simplify information processing. Basically, they're mental shortcuts that can trip us up, leading to inaccurate decision making and erroneous conclusions.

These biases arise from various sources, including our emotions, how we perceive information, and our preexisting beliefs or attitudes. Mind traps, as the name implies, are a form of mental cage or roadblock that can prevent us from achieving our goals, reaching our full potential, or realizing our dreams—you know, all that good stuff we say we want more of!

A mind trap is an information-processing error that occurs when our thought patterns become too rigid or narrow, preventing us from seeing different solutions or alternatives because we are focused on one idea or perspective to the exclusion of all others. We get stuck in these mental loops because our brains are designed to recognize patterns and figure out why things happen. This can be helpful when we're trying to solve problems, but decidedly not when it leads us down the wrong path.

Mind traps don't indicate any weakness or flaw in our character. They're incredibly common and happen to everyone, including the most successful and influential people. They're nothing but glitches in our thinking process that can lead us to perceive events or interactions in a negative, self-deprecating manner, even when all the evidence suggests otherwise.

Recognizing and becoming aware of our mind traps is the first step to overcoming them and living a more fulfilling life. With awareness and understanding, we can learn to see and then break free from these patterns of thinking and create healthier mindsets.

Digging Deeper

When we avoid confronting what makes us afraid by hiding in a mind trap, our amygdalas may feel calm in that moment, and we feel safe temporarily. But ultimately these mind traps hold us back from growing into who we know we can be or from achieving the true emotional connection we desire in our lives. As our self-esteem plummets, so does our courage for taking risks or trying new things.

Many common mind traps are usually influenced by our life stories, such as an unfavorable upbringing, traumatic events, and our perceptions of our own success. When left unchecked, they can lead to negative self-talk and destructive urges just to try to prove our worthiness, leading to feelings of being overwhelmed, stressed, and burdened with anxiety.

HYPERVIGILANCE: HUMMINGBIRDS DON'T RELAX, SO WHY SHOULD I?

More than a few current friends and ex-boyfriends nicknamed me "hummingbird" because I'm rarely seen at rest. Flitting from feeder to bloom and back again all day, from early morning until late at night, I was constantly busy and on the move. Zooming from room to room or task to task, always trying to stay ahead of future problems and planning for every possible danger made me feel safe and in control of a chaotic world. I considered this way of being a superpower because it meant I was always productive.

But in fact, my inability to rest was more about me being stuck in a state of hypervigilance.

Hypervigilance is a state of constant worrying, planning, and preparing for the worst. People who are hypervigilant, like me, see ourselves as prepared for anything—ready to take on whatever bad thing might happen and protect what we love. We're the heroes, ready for every negative eventuality, never letting ourselves relax for even a second. Because if we let our guard down, who knows what might happen?

Hypervigilance makes relaxing physically and emotionally difficult.

For example, I have scoliosis, induced by years of serving tables while putting myself through college. Combined with bending over books and laptops for decades, I have quite the nerd hump. (It's actually called a widow's or dowager's hump, but I find that to be an incredibly sexist term.)

During a pain-relieving massage appointment, while a therapist deftly kneaded my neck and shoulders, she chanted in soothing tones, "Relax. Relax. Just relax."

I tried. I really did.

I did my best to slip into her buttery soft chant and expert touch—but nope. Try as I might, relaxing is just not something I'm good at. The more someone tells me to relax, the less likely I'll find this fabled land of rainbows and unicorns. An inability to relax from hypervigilance keeps you (and me sometimes!) from living a courageous life because it zaps our energy by overtaxing our body and mind.

People who are hypervigilant, like me, see ourselves as prepared for anything—ready to take on whatever bad thing might happen and protect what we love.

If you've ever tried to drive to a new location while listening to the radio, you know how difficult it can be to divide your attention. As Daniel Kahneman put it in *Thinking, Fast and Slow*: "You can do several things at once, but only if they are easy and undemanding." There's a limit to the mental resources we can dedicate to any given task.

We have to be somewhat choosy about the mental paths we walk most often. Our energy and attention are limited resources. If we spend all our cognitive resources on planning for a hypothetical zombie apocalypse, we're left with very little to spend on writing a book (pointing finger at self here). There's just no mental bandwidth left to take risks when you're stuck in a cycle of hypervigilance. Period. If your imagination is so busy keeping you in a state of fear, there is no energy left to take the positive risks that will get you to the future you desire.

STRESSLAXING

There is a man across from me on the plane from Los Angeles to Austin. It is Monday morning, and for this three-hour flight he is set up with an inflatable foot pillow, socks off, and earbuds in—life is good. This dude clearly has an A+ in Relaxing 101. I can't imagine he had a stresslaxing weekend.

Though a relatively new term, "stresslaxing" is just another way of referring to relaxation-induced anxiety, a phenomenon that causes feelings of stress and worry during moments of rest or leisure activities, such as getting a massage or meditating. It's often caused by an overactive mind that can't switch off from stressful thoughts and worries. When attempting to relax, these worries come flooding back in full force, leading to an anxious response, especially if you're in denial about the level of stress you're experiencing in your life overall.

One of the main causes of anxiety in our modern moment is the status symbol of busyness. When you intertwine your personal identity with suffering and struggle (hi, me!), choosing to take care of yourself or even feeling good can be perceived as incredibly dangerous. In a world that increasingly equates busyness with importance, having little time for leisure can signal to others that you deserve a higher social status, under the assumption that the less time we take for ourselves, the more people admire us. As status-building as they may be, job stresses are linked to multiple chronic health issues, including cardiovascular disease, digestive problems, headaches, and mood disorders.

One of the main causes of anxiety in our modern moment is the status symbol of busyness.

Yet it is in the very moments when we try to shed our stresses and relax that our brains sometimes rebel.

PROBLEMATIC PERFECTIONISM

How often do you find yourself thinking, "If it's not perfect, it's not worth doing."

When you can't seem to embrace the idea that "done is better than perfect," problematic perfectionism may be to blame. The idea here is rooted in the deeply held belief that if we look perfect, act perfect, choose perfectly, and live perfectly we'll be perfectly safe. You just need to hit the bull's-eye every time, so you can protect yourself from suffering, so you can be safe from harsh judgment, blame, rejection, and failure.

When my best friend Michelle was in her early thirties, she was chatting with her mom, Momma Kathy, about the perfect time to have kids. Momma Kathy, of course, had the benefit of a lot of wisdom on the subject and said, "Never." Taken aback, Michelle responded, in horror, "You're saying I should never have kids?" Her mom laughed and said, "No, I meant the time will never be perfect. It doesn't matter what the reasons are, but if you wait for perfect, you will always be waiting."

When we wait to share our work or ourselves with the world until perfection is reached, we'll always be waiting. Perfection is desirable because it feels safe. Not that it *is* safe, but it *feels* that way for our amygdalas, which is good enough.

The question is: Does it help or hinder our growth?

Problematic perfectionism is often a tricky beast, disguised as high standards or a dedication to excellence, overachieving, or meticulousness. However, it often masks deeper fears, including fear of failure, fear of being judged, fear of not being enough, fear of criticism, or even the fear of success.

When you're constantly chasing perfection, it's not because you want to be the best. It's because you're afraid of what will happen if you're not. Let's be real, just like fearlessness (see the Fearless Is a Facade chapter 2), perfection is a myth. It doesn't exist. Life is messy, unpredictable, and chaotic.

I get this concept very clearly. I was raised to be perfect—and failed all the time—but as a child, of course, I didn't understand that perfect was impossible. So, when just one of my many to-do list items goes off the rails, I find myself in a full fear-and-shame spiral. I feel worthless, like I have nothing to contribute, that I am obviously a bad person because I forgot to close the kitchen cabinets, again.

By stepping back and applying perspective, it's hard to see how anyone without superpowers could do everything on our modern, never-ending to-do lists, no matter how hard they try.

When you're constantly chasing perfection, it's not because you want to be the best. It's because you're afraid of what will happen if you're not.

Sometimes there's just no controlling traffic or cabinets (I swear they open all by themselves). But since it makes me feel safe, I keep trying, even though the trying is what makes me more fearful. Or it's the fear of failing, of not being enough. Then if things do go wrong, I see it as a reason why I am not good enough. And around the cycle goes.

The first step toward the "done-is-better-than-perfect" lifestyle is recognizing and accepting that it's absolutely acceptable for you to have perfectionist tendencies—and that they're just one of your natural fear responses. It might be your habit to internalize the message that perfectionism is part of who you are, but it's not who you have to be all the time. Mistakes are opportunities for growth, not reflections of your worth.

If you struggle with problematic perfectionism, would you be open to experimenting with letting go of that sense of control slowly? By maybe leaving in all the extra exclamation points in the email to the team or walking away from your unmade bed. Or, for those recovering perfectionists, go an entire day wearing mismatched socks.

COURAGE QUEST: Problematic Perfectionism

In what areas of your life do you find yourself obsessing over every little detail? In what areas of your life do you adhere to "done is better than perfect"?

Do any of these resonate with you?

Fear of Failure: You're so afraid of failing that you set impossibly high standards for yourself. You'd rather not try at all than try and fail.

Fear of Judgment: You're afraid of what people might think or say about you. So you try to be perfect to avoid any potential criticism.

Fear of Uncertainty: You are driven to control as much as possible. You fear the unpredictability of outcomes, so you strive to perfect every variable within your reach.

Can you describe a time when you were so fixated on getting everything just right that you missed a deadline or scrapped the project entirely?

Do you find yourself avoiding challenges because you're afraid of not being "perfect"?

Are you overly critical of yourself? Do you beat yourself up for minor mistakes?

Just know that you don't have to exhaust yourself to be loved, to be enough.

FEAR OF FAILURE (OR SUCCESS)

The fear of failure is an incredibly common phenomenon. It occurs when you're so afraid to make mistakes or take risks that you become paralyzed and frozen. People may also experience fear of failure if they've had past experiences where they failed at something and were traumatized by the experience.

The fear of failure can be particularly detrimental when pursuing your dreams or achieving your goals. When faced with a challenge, it can feel easier to just give up before even starting, rather than experiencing the potential disappointment that comes with failing. On the flip side, many people also suffer from a fear of success—that achieving your goals will bring more responsibility than you want or can handle. This is especially true for those who have achieved a certain level of success and now feel overwhelmed by the pressure to maintain their performance level or stay on top.

In a study that zeroed in on students' fear of failure and the associated discomfort, Rebecca Cox, researcher and author of the book *The College Fear Factor*, found that when faced with a fear of failure—not actual failure—students reacted in one of four common ways:

1. They slightly avoided their fear of failing the course by putting off the coursework until the last minute;

2. They entirely avoided their fear by ignoring all coursework and assignments;

3. They moved away or scaled back from the course to make the work (and their fear) feel more manageable; or

4. They reframed their fear of failure to be more of a motivator than a deterrent.

Personally, I naturally gravitate toward options 1 through 3, but research shows that those who reported choosing option 4 were less anxious and more successful.

Because the fear of failure can arise during myriad circumstances, it can be tricky to figure out why you feel this way. Variables like your upbringing can make you more susceptible to fear of failure if those influential in your young life, including parents and teachers, were critical, unsupportive, and had unrealistic expectations. Previous traumatic events also influence your future trepidation around failure. For example, if you got sick on stage during your last big speech, you may be scared of the same thing happening again.

And, of course, failure looks different for everyone.

Regularly being fearful of failure can prevent you from trying new things and taking advantage of opportunities. Avoidance (see page 123) may also be commonly paired with fear of failure, as you refuse to learn new things, meet new people, or get involved. Fear of failure can also color how you see yourself, often causing you to engage in negative self-talk that affects your self-esteem and self-confidence. As a result, you may self-sabotage with actions that undermine your progress toward a goal.

Next time you find yourself mired in the fear of failure, try to redefine that imagined worst-case scenario as an opportunity or an experiment instead of a hindrance.

Like the students who made their fear a motivator, try to reframe what failure is in your mind. Are your expectations for yourself too high? Or are you simply thinking about failure in an unhelpful way? Next time you find yourself mired in the fear of failure, try to redefine that imagined worst-case scenario as an opportunity or an experiment instead of a hindrance. Removing a potential failure's power by actively reframing it can help you manage your fears and motivate you to move forward with your goals.

IMPOSTER SYNDROME

Have you ever worked really hard for something, but still felt like a fraud? Perhaps you've achieved something remarkable, yet felt like it was all just a stroke of luck or good timing. If so, you're not alone.

Imposter syndrome refers to the tendency of individuals who are highly accomplished to downplay their achievements and attribute them to external factors, like networking, charm, or being in the right place at the right time. According to a 2011 study, 70 percent of the general public reported struggling with imposter syndrome. Despite their undeniable success, people wrestling with this syndrome constantly feel like imposters, doubting their abilities and fearing that they will be exposed as frauds. This mindset not only poses a challenge to your self-perception but also hinders your ability to fully embrace or celebrate your accomplishments.

My journey with imposter syndrome began the moment I decided to go to college.

It was the summer between seventh and eighth grade, and I thought it was a good idea to make some summer cash by getting a job on a blueberry farm. Pickers were paid by each bucket filled, and in my child's mind blueberries were quite small, so I thought it would be easy.

I lasted exactly one day.

I can vividly recall sweating under the midday sun, looking down at my woefully meager pickings. I had the scratches on my hands to prove I was trying but getting absolutely nowhere with filling enough blueberry buckets for the day to even buy lunch.

Momma Helen didn't find my desire to try blueberry picking at twelve years old odd because our family was firmly planted in the blue-collar working class. Born to a teenage mom and adopted at birth by my maternal grandmother who raised four other kids who didn't graduate high school didn't exactly position me for a college degree. In fact, no one in my family had even tried to pursue higher education. We were a family of truck drivers and assembly line workers, and part of me thought that was just the way of things.

But under that scorching sun, faced with the reality of how physically grueling life would be on the path that my family had chosen, I knew I wanted something different, something bigger.

Fast-forward to my first day of university. Overwhelmed and mesmerized with the sights and sounds of a real college campus and being a real college student, I didn't notice the six-foot construction trench . . . until I fell into it. Just like it was ripped from a coming-of-age college rom-com movie, my dirt-covered body had to be pulled up by a few of my new classmates. Although it was the first hole in college I fell into, it wasn't the last. Future holes were more of the metaphorical type and full of feeling like an imposter who didn't really deserve to be there.

Although I didn't have these words for it at the time, I tried to minimize the dread of being an imposter with perfectionism and being the hardest worker in the room, no matter the cost to my physical or mental health. In a seemingly never-ending cycle, I grappled with worry, self-doubt, and anxiety whenever given a project or task, which I dealt with by either overpreparing or procrastinating.

On the other side, if I got positive feedback, I would ignore, deflect, or dismiss it. Part of me felt guilty for working in a temperature-controlled lab while others in my family were in sweltering, difficult conditions. I thought if I just worked long enough and hard enough, others would start to see me as enough, so I could then see myself as enough. I thought I could outrun my worries, but alas, we can't ever outrun ourselves.

The clouds of my imposter syndrome finally broke when I did one of the most embarrassing things of my life up to that point. On my first day at my dream job at NASA's Ames Research Center Moffett Field, I was so caught up in my own thoughts of not belonging and not being good enough (despite the evidence of literally being hired at NASA), I hit my new manager's car.

Let me repeat. I hit my new manager's car on my first day at NASA! (yeesh)

With my music loud enough to drown out my fears of inadequacy, I accidentally backed into my manager's car in the parking lot. To make matters worse, I was so preoccupied with my thoughts of not being good enough for NASA and analyzing all my perceived missteps that day that I didn't even realize it. Caught on security camera, I had to be contacted by senior leadership to sort out a hit-and-run situation. On my first day.

I was mortified and knew something had to change. I had to change.

Of course, there was no "poof" moment that made me never feel like an imposter again. But it was definitely a turning point in my life: either I continued to wallow in my perceptions of where I belonged or I found ways to deal with the chatty demons of my endless internal monologue so I could live the life I wanted to live.

How to Avoid Goodbyes

It began on a placid Tuesday night. After helping Momma Helen on her nightly slow shuffle down the short hallway and back, I turned in—exhausted—at 7:00 p.m. I had quickly learned that taking care of an aging parent is much like taking care of a baby: When they sleep, you sleep. Back then, my life was a game of survival.

That night, I awoke to my mother's screams: "MARY! MARY!"

I've never been a gentle waker-upper. I'm the sort whose eyelids fly open at the hint of sound or light. I had so many recurring nightmares of my mom screaming my name they may have matched the actual number of nights she did it, so it took me a moment to grab hold of reality.

Unfortunately, this particular scream was not a dream—it was from just across the hallway. I barrel-rolled out of bed, my mind well behind my feet. It was not the first time I'd been awakened like this.

As I'd done many times before, I called the doctor on duty, who then called an ambulance. The medics rushed into our tiny living room and, with her pink cotton nightgown flapping against the gurney, rolled her away.

The ER doctor asked me to sit, then cleared his throat in the way people do before they're about to change your life: "I think it's time you make a decision. A decision . . ." he trailed off. "A decision on whether or not we should continue to do any drastic life-saving procedures or we should let her finally rest."

All the anger and irritation at being inconvenienced with yet another middle-of-the-night trip to the ER washed away as I began to ask every question I knew to ask until he finally said, "Of course, it is your choice. But I think the kinder choice is to let her go."

Having lost the ability to form more words in that moment, I nodded in assent, to which he replied, "I'll just need your signature here."

"Wait, what? I need to sign my mother's death warrant like a credit card slip at the end of the night?"

COURAGE QUEST:
Imposter Syndrome

Key signs of imposter syndrome:

Are you afraid of being exposed as unworthy?

Do you find yourself apologizing even when you're not at fault?

Do you think others place too much importance on your achievements?

Do you fear that your true inadequacies will be discovered by others?

When you experience success, do you dismiss it as mere luck or deflect the spotlight to others?

Do you believe that others perceive your success as greater than it actually is?

In hindsight I realize the legal need for such things, but in my defense it was three o'clock in the morning, I had had very little sleep, and I was now being asked to sign away someone's life. And not just someone, but the only person I had ever called Mom.

Perhaps I had waited a bit longer than was proper because the doctor cleared his throat again. I bit back the urge to say something I'd regret later. Instead of hiding my fear with aggression and anger, I took the thirty-cent blue pen from his hand and signed Momma Helen's life away in triplicate.

I nodded my thanks to the staff and shuffled out of the empty waiting room into the predawn morning. In the front seat of my Mazda 3, I grabbed the wheel and ugly cried until the sun shone over Niles Canyon. I knew it was the right decision. My mother had been so sick she could barely walk or eat for weeks. There was no hope of her recovering, so I made the painful decision to let her go and took on the mantle of responsibility for it being "my fault," for "not doing enough," for "not being enough" for years while I learned, unlearned, and created the neurohacks I'll share with you here.

The waves of loss and her eventual death felt natural. What felt shameful at the time was the overwhelming sense of peace and freedom I felt. It had been a very lonely two years of being her only caretaker—from hospitals to surgeries to around-the-clock meds and wound care—all while pretending everything was just fine, lecturing to my students with nothing but smiles so I could keep my mom and me financially afloat. And now that was all over. My entire world was about to change—and I could see cracks in the cage bars starting to show.

The long night in the emergency room turned into three short days waiting for nature to take its course. My best friend Michelle and her newborn daughter Maddie held vigil with me while I clattered about packing and sorting, washing away my anxiety in Clorox wipes and wine. If my hands were busy, I didn't have to think about the emotional implications of what was happening just down the hallway. Of what I had just done. If I was being productive, I didn't have to feel anger or hurt or sadness.

If I was busy, I didn't have to say goodbye.

Then the time came. I approached Momma Helen's bedside feeling like there was a thunderstorm coming my way, knowing it would be a memory I would return to for the rest of my life. Tears streamed down my face as she and I sat there in silence, hand-in-hand, until she finally let go with one final deep guttural whoosh. With tears welling in my eyes, I stroked her soft skin one last time and said goodbye so I could get back to the kitchen and clean away my heartache, sorrow, and fear of what would come next.

Avoidance: How We Keep Our Fear Cages Strong

Avoidance is a tactic that many of us use to put off an action or a task that makes us feel afraid.

For me, avoidance manifests as near-obsessive house cleaning. For example, my house absolutely sparkled while I was writing my doctoral dissertation on fear and courage. Chapters due to my major adviser? Oops, looks like my kitchen cabinets need a thorough scrub. Word messed up all my formatting? Looks like I need to clean the inside of my oven . . . again.

Cleaning makes me feel in control, like I'm enough. Vacuuming the floors for the fifth time in a week helps me feel useful and safe from my fear of failure. I'll scrub the water spots on my bathroom mirror before tackling that deadline hanging over me or making that important phone call. Or convince myself I'm not procrastinating because it had to be done anyway at some point, so now I'll really be able to focus!

Cleaning is my cardio.

But the truth is, after two hours of cleaning I'm worn out, and all I want to do is recline with a YA novel featuring a magical talking cat. When we avoid confronting the thing that makes us afraid by doing something else instead, we tell ourselves that we're really taking action, which calms our amygdala and makes us feel safe. And feeling safe feels good! But alas, as my favorite fridge magnet says, what you want is on the other side of fear.

I could write an entire book on the ways I've avoided discomfort in my life—and I bet you could too. Cleaning isn't the only avoidance technique I've employed. After my mom died, I found it too difficult to deal with those big emotions, so I fled the country. I gave away all my stuff except what could fit in two suitcases and a five-by-five-foot storage unit and moved from the San Francisco Bay Area to London, where I didn't know a soul.

Staying in California, where I grew up, felt dangerous—not because I was in physical danger, but because all the ghosts of my past were there. The seven blocks I would circle as a high school transfer student to avoid eating by myself in the cafeteria. The Outback Steakhouse where my (now) ex-husband worked when we were in college and where I would meet him for margaritas after his shift. The emergency room where I had to sign the consent to let my mom pass from this world to the next. It was all too much.

Fleeing to a new country and new city with no memories felt incredibly safe and action-packed—two things my amygdala loved! Dealing with a litany of logistics meant I could avoid dealing with my emotional turmoil.

Bravery Break: TMI: Trigger, Mind Chatter, Improve

This neurohack was created as an updated refresh on a few classic cognitive behavioral therapy (CBT) techniques, including the ABC model and Catch, Challenge, Release.

To help deepen your understanding, strengthen your anterior cingulate cortex (ACC, "The Mediator" part of your brain), and create actionable steps for improvement, follow these steps next time you catch yourself in a stressful experience. In the context of fear, the ACC aids in regulating emotional responses and plays a crucial role in the processing and permanent storage of our frightening memories. The ACC is incredibly unique because it has physical connections to both the "cognitive" prefrontal cortex and the "emotional" amygdala.

It's best to jot these down, but even going through the steps mentally is valuable.

Step 1: Trigger
Describe the activating event that triggered your fear response.

Step 2: Mind Chatter
In the moment, detail what you're thinking, feeling, or doing while you're experiencing a particular trigger. It doesn't need to be perfect. Just jot down anything you're saying to yourself, thinking about, reacting to, or noticing—such as, for example, you're repeating a long-held belief like "I'm no good at . . ." or "I always . . ."

Step 3: Improve
Without overthinking it, name exactly one thing you could improve right now that would lessen the trigger itself or the mind chatter that comes after.

Moving to London was the balm my soul needed, but it didn't fix any of the underlying issues, which I would discover after falling in love with a man in a piano bar on a rainy night in South Kensington—and then moving to Los Angeles a year later to end the bicontinental shuffle that Craig and I had been doing.

Although we were happy together, living together in the same house felt like locking myself into a new cage. Same city? Yes! Same house? No, thanks. In fact, I refused to buy any bulky furniture for my new Los Angeles bungalow. Formerly part of the servants' quarters for film legend Jean Harlow, it was small enough that I didn't need much to furnish it. Other than a bed and a couch, I only bought furniture that I could quickly fold up and pack flat, because being able to pick up and leave at a moment's notice made me feel safe and in control.

Working and living out of a suitcase as a digital nomad gave me the liberation I desperately craved after feeling trapped by my mother's illness and being her sole caretaker. That dream of working remote from London, Paris, or Sydney was what sustained me through hours of working remote from a laptop in a hospital waiting room. In that time, I began to see attachment as dangerous. Committing to anything permanent, even if it was just a piece of furniture, was to be avoided at all costs. "Disposable" meant I wouldn't be too disappointed if I had to leave it behind one day. Whether it was furniture, people, or places, I could avoid the pain that often came with committing to something besides myself. Or so I thought.

My fear of commitment, and thus true connection, was so intense that I was avoiding anything and everything that might be considered putting down roots.

This type of avoidance is just one of many mind traps we can fall into as we try to sort out the hardest parts of our lives.

Don't Should All Over Yourself

Our brains love to categorize. We can't help it. Often this means that we classify nuanced ideas or complex experiences into one of two boxes. For example, my go-to self-deprecation is that I am a black-thumbed biologist because I can't keep any plants alive, especially in my own house. The story I always told myself is "I'm not a plant person."

That all changed when one of my best friends, Stephanie, a green-thumbed plant devotee, texted me entirely too early one spring Saturday morning, asking if I wanted to go with her to a members-only plant sale at Huntington Gardens in Los Angeles. I raised an eyebrow, confused about what a members-only plant sale was. Stephanie guaranteed it would be fun, so off we went. But I assured her I wouldn't be buying anything because I am an inveterate plant killer.

At the garden we perused the greenery for sale, all tended with care by volunteers who waxed poetic about their chlorophylled children, some actually showing pictures of them as seedlings. Then Stephanie turned to me and said, "Pick a plant—you're going home with something; I'm buying."

"It just seems sadistic," I protested. "I always kill plants—I can never keep them alive. I absolutely should not be a plant mom."

With an expression that welcomed no rebuke, she said, "Don't should all over yourself."

"Should" statements refer to a set of conditions or options that a person believes they should or shouldn't meet. Other versions of "should" statements include "must" or "ought to." These thoughts often cause guilt when we do not meet the conditions. Plus, if we place "should" statements on other people, we often feel anger and resentment. When we lock ourselves into a never-ending list of "shoulds" and "musts," we become afraid to act, explore, and, especially, take risks.

After barking out a laugh, I paused to ingest Stephanie's words when she asked, "What can you do right now to change the story in your head?"

After a brief moment, I awkwardly said, "Well . . . I'm good at keeping my animals alive and I name all my pets, so . . . maybe . . . I name the plant?"

COURAGE QUEST: Automatic Thoughts

Automatic thinking refers to images or thoughts that occur naturally in our minds in response to triggers. These thoughts or images are instantaneous and not consciously drawn—they stem from our beliefs and thoughts about ourselves and the world around us. And they often occur based on habits that we've formed and information we've previously learned. This automatic thinking can affect our moods, emotions, and behaviors.

Common negative automatic thoughts include statements like "I'm worthless," "I'm a failure," "I'm no good," or "Everyone hates me."

Examining your thoughts this way allows you to determine what responses might be more accurate, adaptive, or positive. From there, you can work on increasing courage by developing positive affirmations to use when experiencing negative automatic thinking. A good exercise for managing automatic thinking is to write out your thoughts, feelings, and responses. Questioning the accuracy of your automatic thinking and practicing positive slogans can train your brain toward more accurate thinking.

When you catch yourself in a negative automatic thought, pause and ask:

- What exact details or evidence makes this thought true?

- Is there another explanation or another way of looking at the situation?

- What would I tell a friend or loved one who was having this thought?

- What is a possible positive replacement for this negative automatic thought? Can you craft a replacement similar to "I am valued, I am loved," "I'm a fighter," "I am good enough," or "I would rather be a few people's shot of whiskey than everyone's cup of tea"?

"Perfect!" she yelled, loudly clapping her hands together. "Let's go find your new plant baby!"

As we meandered the garden, I thought to myself, "How does one name a bloody plant?" No sooner than I had finished that thought, I turned the corner and found the cutest little peachy pink miniature rose tree with "Cutie Pie" emblazed in gold sharpie across its black pot. For better or worse, I loaded Cutie Pie onto our flatbed cart and wheeled it to its new life, or tragic death.

Driving home with Cutie Pie's leaves flapping in the windy top-down backseat of Stephanie's convertible, I dove deeper into the benefits of challenging my long-held mind trap. Not that I had dreams of becoming a talented gardener, but when we practice rewriting one cognitive distortion, we get better at rewriting them all.

Retraining our brain works best with diverse lessons spread out over time.

It's now been two years since bringing Cutie Pie home, and I'm happy to say she's still alive! Like plants weathering seasons and storms, we too can grow, change, and bloom.

FOCUS ON NEGATIVES OVER POSITIVES

On a recent trip to Panama, I fell in a hole nearly the exact size of my foot, broke two toes, and got a grade 3 sprain. This experience really tracked well for my perfectionism, since grade 3 is the most serious level of ankle sprain and you can't really be a true perfectionist unless you're willing to go for the highest score in all things.

The injury happened after Craig and I had taken a catamaran tour to this tiny island with exactly one road going east to west and one north to south. The village, with only a handful of thatch-roofed shops, had no dock or marina, so we swam about two football fields distance to shore. After checking out the village, we began walking back and I was so distracted by the breathtaking views that I didn't notice the hole in the road. And fell right into it.

Based on the twist and the crack, I knew it was bad. I was livid, so angry at myself for making the grave error of gazing upon idyllic tropical waters. I mean, who does that? Only a troglodyte, clearly.

I berated myself all the way back to the beach and cursed between breaths on my one-legged swim back to the catamaran. For the entire way home and for months afterward, the injury colored the entire trip as awful, leaving me to vow that I would never return to Panama.

When I fell, I zeroed in on that brief moment of strife and applied it to the entire trip. I even began to go back over the week to find other "negative" moments to help justify my indignation and reinforce why it was all Panama's fault.

DOUBLE STANDARDS

Double standards are about holding yourself accountable for things you wouldn't dream of holding others accountable for. For example, if it were Craig who fell into the hole in Panama, I would've never considered it a failure on his part. I would've seen it as an unfortunate accident and moved on. However, in my case, I held myself to such an unachievable standard of perfection that I internalized the accident as a failing on my part. Clearly, I wasn't good enough to sidestep the hole and avoid injury.

BREAKING FREE FROM OUR MIND TRAP CAGES

Often, our greatest battles are those that take place within the confines of our own minds.

By spotting our fear-influenced thinking patterns and understanding their root causes, we can start building bridges away from those invisible fear cages that keep us trapped.

Broadly speaking, the cognitive distortions explored in this chapter are patterns of thought that cause us to misperceive our reality. They are habitual ways of thinking that are often inaccurate and negatively biased and not indicative of a person's intelligence or education level.

Recognizing these distortions can be crucial in both challenging and changing harmful thought patterns, leading to a braver and more fulfilling life. They can also be tricky to spot, as they're often deeply ingrained in our thought processes. But with knowledge, awareness, and practice, they can be recognized and corrected.

By spotting our fear-influenced thinking patterns and understanding their root causes, we can start building bridges away from those invisible fear cages that keep us trapped. The key is understanding what's holding us back. Once we figure that part out, we can work on developing strategies (hint: keep reading) to navigate through them.

The good news is that you don't have to stay stuck in your fears forever. By choosing to dive deeper, you're taking control of your narrative. You're choosing courage over comfort and growth over fear. Go you!

PART THREE

The Keys to Courage

CHAPTER 8

Set Yourself Free with the RAIN Method

Fear is a difficult thing to let go of, but I'm willing to try.
—*THE MORTAL WORD* BY GENEVIEVE COGMAN

One of my superpowers is making connections between things that, on the surface, look disparate but in fact can be combined into something new and even revolutionary.

Neurohacking combines principles from neurobiology and psychology to help you develop resilience and strength in challenging situations. In doing so, you can create lasting changes in how you think, feel, and behave. Neurohacking can also help you gain greater control over your emotions, allowing you to better navigate through the myriad ways that fear expresses itself, building stronger courage muscles in the process.

I developed the idea of neurohacking when I was first researching fear and courage. I simply couldn't find a practice that housed the tools needed to better navigate our everyday, totally normal feelings of unease, nervousness, or foreboding. Also, many of the skills and tools that are part of my neurohacks were buried deep in academic journal articles, which are a chore to read and often completely inaccessible to people outside of research and development institutions because of the outlandish paywalls created by publishers (fun fact: academic researchers make zero dollars from writing and publishing their research in scientific journals).

I created the RAIN method—which stands for Recognize, Assign, Identify, and Navigate—because I wanted to have a fully accessible, easy-to-remember (and use!) framework to deal with everyday fear, one that included multiple coping skills and was customizable for each person's unique brain.

Rooted in published research of mine and others, the RAIN method is a composite process I designed based on tried-and-true foundations for fighting the debilitating feelings of fear while strengthening our courage muscles. Like all the neurohacks shared in this book, the RAIN method will not hurt you and is free to do, so play around with it, experiment, try it on for size.

When I was in high school in the mid-1990s, I learned about these magical little yellow-and-black booklets called *CliffsNotes*. Their existence was passed along in hushed whispers because, essentially, as millions discovered before me, these were cheat codes for all the classics we had to read at the time. Since the internet was barely a thing then, *CliffsNotes* were an incredible shortcut to get our "boring" reading done.

Looking back through my current lens as an academic, a teacher, I can see that by using *CliffsNotes* I cheated myself out of the full experience of these important works. But these cheat codes allowed me to get through an overwhelming number of dense texts, leaving me with a better understanding of the broad strokes.

Which is to say that neurohacks are like *CliffsNotes*. They aren't meant to solve every problem nor give you the full, detailed, word-for-word experience. They're shortcuts to get you to the other side of fear quicker and with less suffering. I found that when I could move quickly through feelings of being stuck, frozen, or wanting to run the other way, I had the confidence and energy to do the things I always dreamed of. This included boldly arguing with a customs agent in El Salvador who tried to shake me down for extra "fees." Or having the belief in myself that even when my courage muscles are exhausted from a season of challenges, I know I can build them back stronger than ever.

Neurohacks help me feel confident that I can handle my distressing sensations in the moment, and that I will have a set of tools to use, add to, and build a future full of freedom, connection, and adventure.

The Four Steps of the RAIN Method

The RAIN method—recognize, assign, identify, and navigate—systematically lays out a four-step process for changing your perception of, and experience with, everyday fears.

Here's how RAIN works:

1. **Recognize:** In this first step, take a moment to acknowledge and name the physical aspects you experience when entering a state of fear arousal. For me, my tells are scrunching shoulders, dry mouth (I drink a lot of water when speaking on stage!), and a noticeably increased heart rate. I say noticeable because although the fear-arousal response will generally always include this, we're not all actively aware of the shift. Your tells could be clenching your jaw, quicker breathing, or sweaty palms.

2. **Assign:** Once you've identified that you're in a state of fear arousal, you can assign a name to the emotion that has emerged in response to a particular trigger. The Fear Wheel

(see page 142) can be a wonderful tool for this. Then allow that emotion to exist without negative judgment.

For example, it took me decades to be able to sit in my feelings of overwhelm and not drag shame to the party. Craig, my partner, might even argue, with a thirty-two-slide presentation, that it was writing this book that truly allowed me to feel powerful while simultaneously feeling overwhelmed. I tend to feel overwhelmed when I'm pushing myself to do something new, something vulnerable. But it is also stuff that is worthwhile and important, even when it's hard. By choosing just one word to label our emotional experience in the moment, we can bring some logical perspective to our current experience instead of thoughtlessly being swept away by it.

3. **Identify:** Look deeper into your fear by asking yourself questions such as "Where is this sensation coming from?" and "What are my thoughts or beliefs around this feeling?" These questions allow you to categorize your fear as one of two fundamental types: the fear of not being enough or of losing control. By investigating and categorizing the root of our fearful thoughts and feelings, we can derail the discomfort that accompanies a heightened state of fear arousal.

4. **Navigate:** Finally, once you've recognized, assigned, and identified your fears, it's time to put your favorite neurohacks into action.

The steps in the RAIN Method—recognize, assign, identify, and navigate—are meant to be carried out in order whenever you sense that you're having a fear reaction. The first three steps of RAIN are about observing, articulating, and classifying your physical (biological reactions) and emotional experiences, while the last step is about using neurohacks to navigate through the discomfort.

4 Steps for neutralizing FICTIONAL FEAR

1 RECOGNIZE

Racing Heart

Dry Mouth

Foggy Thinking

Faster Breathing

Sweaty/Clammy Skin

Digestive Issues

2 ASSIGN

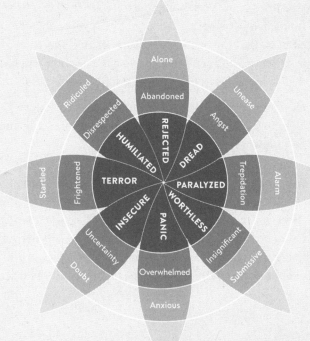

Fear can initially be divided into two buckets: **factual** and **fictional**. Factual fear is in the moment, actual physical threats to your survival or those you care for. Fictional fear is the response we have to everything else that "stresses" us out.

3

IDENTIFY

Most of our stress is actually fear that can be grossly categorized into one of two commonly shared fears. In the moment, ask yourself which one of these are you responding to?

4

NAVIGATE

This step can be any of your favorite tools or techniques, like box breathing.

STEP 1: RECOGNIZE (THE "FEEL IT" STAGE)

Your body is a powerful indicator of your emotions, even those that you may not be able to acknowledge openly. The first step of the RAIN method brings awareness to your feelings of fear as soon as possible so you can begin to address them before your amygdala sends you into a spiral. This small act of self-reflection provides critical distance from the uncomfortable sensations because it automatically switches your "thinking brain" back on.

Some of the more common physiological responses to fear arousal are a racing heart, dry mouth, foggy thinking, faster breathing, sweaty palms, and digestive distress. But your particular set of physical responses may vary. I tend to scrunch my shoulders and clench my jaw when faced with mild fear-based distress, and if things reach a moderate level my mouth goes dry. When I notice any of these "tells," I know it's time to get curious about what's triggering my fear response.

Which of these are your tells?

- Nausea/indigestion, sometimes described as "butterflies"

- Sweating and/or chills

- Diarrhea

- Dizziness

- Tense or trembling muscles, especially in the shoulders and jaw

- Racing heart

- Shortness of breath or faster breathing

- Chest pain

- Dry mouth

- Feeling "frozen" or paralyzed

- Disassociation or feeling like you're watching what's happening from outside of yourself

Although you've likely experienced one or more of these physical reactions in moments of stress, you may not have always recognized that they're related to your body's fear-arousal response. That's why the "recognize" stage of the RAIN method is so important—it alerts you to your body's fear response and directs you to observe it with curiosity and acceptance instead of judgment or criticism. The aim with the recognize stage is to simply acknowledge the fact that you're afraid without trying to push it away or deny it.

The aim with the recognize stage is to simply acknowledge the fact that you're afraid without trying to push it away or deny it.

If you're not used to tracking symptoms of stress in your body, it can be tough to recognize them at first. Many of us get used to those knots in our shoulders or to frequent stomach upsets, never equating these bodily discomforts to a fear response. It takes a bit of practice and repetition to build the habits needed to recognize your fear symptoms every time, so the Courage Quest: Fear Tracker that follows (see page 144) may help. Just as every good poker player must know their "tells," you should know what your body does when it starts to enter its fear zone.

Turtle or porcupine: How do you react when you're afraid?

When people feel threatened, they usually respond in one of two ways—they "quill out" like a porcupine, trying to out-scare the thing that's scaring them, or they hide like a turtle, withdrawing into their shell. If it feels overwhelming to keep track of your fear "tells," start by noticing if you're a porcupine or a turtle.

When faced with a challenge or setback, porcupines will get loud and angry, using bravado to feel more powerful and less vulnerable. The coworker who hides their feelings of inadequacy by storming out of a meeting after their idea is passed on, or the parent who yells at their kids when they're worried about money, are examples of porcupines.

Turtles, on the other hand, go inward. They pull back, try to get as small as possible, and wait for the turbulence to pass. This can look like a total shutdown, disinterest, or disengagement from the outside. Those who naturally turtle when confronted with a tense or difficult situation are sometimes perceived as being agreeable or complacent when, in fact, they're trying to return to safety by disengaging from the moment. For turtles, the quickest way to feel safe again is to become practically invisible.

STEP 2: ASSIGN (THE "NAME IT TO TAME IT" STAGE)

Beetlejuice! Rumpelstiltskin!

There is power in naming things. We see it in storytelling, pop culture, and marketing. Plenty of my favorite young adult supernatural novels are built on the idea that if you know the name of the elf, faerie, or demon, you can control it.

If you name it, you can tame it.

The second step is to assign a name or label to the fear you're experiencing. This makes it easier to identify and differentiate between types of fears. It can also help you start to uncover the underlying beliefs, patterns, and stories that might be fueling your fear. Sometimes, just naming it can short-circuit a fear response.

To help with this, I created the "Fear Wheel," based on American psychologist and researcher Robert Plutchik's "Wheel of Emotions."

When faced with a challenge or setback, porcupines will get loud and angry, using bravado to feel more powerful and less vulnerable.

As a professor at the Albert Einstein College of Medicine, Plutchik has authored or co-authored more than 260 articles, forty-five chapters, and eight books on the study of emotions. His Wheel of Emotions was created as a visual guide to help us better understand the depth and breadth of our emotional spectrum. He wanted to create a tangible map of the rocky terrain of our eight primary emotions: fear, trust, anger, joy, sadness, disgust, anticipation, and surprise. (There are different schools of thought that believe there are really only four: happiness, sadness, fear, and anger.) Regardless of which you choose, these core emotions mix together like primary-colored paints to create all the varying shades of our emotional spectrum.

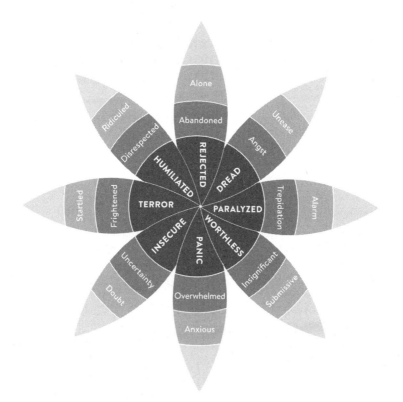

Generally speaking there are three basic categories of how we can describe our emotional state in words: subjective, behavioral, and functional. Since the goal of the Fear Wheel is to disengage our amygdala, not overwhelm it further, I chose to use the simplest of the three, subjective. However, it's still valid to describe your emotional experience by describing how you behave during that feeling or how you functionally relate that feeling to the effects of the emotion on your environment.

For example, instead of just using the word "fear" to describe a time when you felt afraid, you could describe the event as you withdrawing or escaping from the trigger. Or, if you were more interested in using functional language, you could describe the event as you "being driven to protect yourself."

I adapted Plutchick's Wheel of Emotions to a fear-based set of emotions to help you zero in on the many nuances of how *you*

COURAGE QUEST:
Fear Tracker

When you write down your anxious thoughts, you gain insight into their origins and meaning, allowing you to visualize a new, bolder future. Journaling can also help you process difficult emotions like fear, because when you write down what you're feeling and reflect on it, you become more aware of negative thought patterns that contribute to it. Once you recognize those patterns you can challenge them, develop healthier coping skills, and replace them with more positive thinking to improve your mental health.

To begin to see patterns in how you experience and navigate everyday fear, try keeping a log of any anxious thoughts or fearful feelings that come up during the day—either digitally or physically.

If you prefer a little more structure to your journaling, try using this format:

Date:

Triggering event:

Level of intensity (mild, moderate, severe):

Physical responses noticed:

How you responded to the trigger:

Do you wish you had responded differently? If so, how?

experience fear. By using the Fear Wheel as a tool, suddenly the unknown becomes knowable.

And since we experience emotions on a spectrum of intensity, you will find some words more extreme than others by design. With the help of the Fear Wheel, you can transform your distress from an amorphous dark cloud swirling around your head to something solid you can grab onto and study to understand it better.

When using the Fear Wheel, you're able to pause your runaway emotions to take a moment for awareness, which is key to de-escalating your amygdala's fear response. The Fear Wheel allows your brain to put feelings into designated categories, which our brains love. Because we fear losing control, we thrive on organization and categorization. By naming how you feel and putting that feeling into a "box" in your brain, you can relax because you feel you've regained control. Then figuring out what to do next suddenly becomes a lot easier.

Decoding our emotional complexity

Many of us don't even know when we're feeling afraid because fear is so repressed in Western society. The

Fear Wheel removes the layers of denial and repression between you and your fear, reinforcing your natural ability to recognize when you're feeling fear so you can respond accordingly.

But the real power of the Fear Wheel is that it gives you explicit permission to be afraid. Once you've whipped out the Fear Wheel, the emotion is already on the table. Why not then just accept it, even welcome it? An added bonus of the Fear Wheel is that it's private and powerful. I recommend having

By assigning a specific name to your fear, you solidify the experience you're having.

it saved as an image on your phone, so it's always handy. (You can download one at https://marypoffenroth.com/bravenewyou.)

By assigning a specific name to your fear, you solidify the experience you're having. This allows you to move forward instead of remaining in the stormy realm of your feelings. This is an important step in the RAIN process. When you name your experience, you allow yourself to explore it further, which is much better than simply ignoring it or pretending it doesn't exist.

Emotions are not isolated phenomena—they often exist in relation to one another. Articulating your internal experience accurately, especially when you're feeling complex, difficult feelings, can seem impossible. The Fear Wheel is here to help simplify the description process for you. Use this tool to gain insight into your emotional makeup and bolster your ability to effectively communicate your emotional experiences to yourself and others.

STEP 3: IDENTIFY (THE "SORT IT" STAGE)

After completing Steps 1 and 2, if you're still feeling distressed ask yourself the following: Into which of the two fear buckets does my fear fall? The fear of not being enough or the fear of not being in control?

The bulk of our fictional fears (see page 10) can be put into one of these basic categories. And while some experiences are so complex that they contain a little bit of both, for the identify step, to pull

Bravery Break: The Smell of Courage

Looking for another option besides box breathing for the navigate step of the RAIN process?

Since aromas travel through the nose and directly into our brains via our olfactory system, the impact on the amygdala is nearly immediate. When we experience detectable scents, our olfactory system is stimulated, resulting in either no fear-arousal response or a marked increase or decrease in it. Feeling more relaxed or more stressed will depend on the chemical makeup of the substance and your personal association with the smell. Specifically, breathing in oils from lavender, cypress, and thyme has been empirically shown, at the molecular level, to have a stress-suppressing effect on stress-responsive biomarkers.

Biomarkers are objective clues to what's happening in your mind or body. Unlike symptoms you can describe as "I feel X," or "it hurts in Y," which rely solely on our personal perceptions, biomarkers are measurable evidence, like this morning's outdoor temperature, that remain observable even from an outsider's perspective. Not to discount anyone's personal experience, of course, but biomarkers serve as an additional tool to understand the complexity of our human suffering.

How does all this translate to fear? Certain strong smells can help bring fast relief to anxiety, allowing us to interrupt an activated amygdala, de-escalate our stress response, and return to a sense of calm.

Personally, I use the essential oils mentioned here in a slim roller ball bottle that I can easily fit in any tiny pocket (you want to use the essential oils because you need the smell to be *strong*!). Before I go on stage or into a high-stress environment, I pop the cap and roll a little of the pungent oil under my nose and around my nostrils. Often I feel immediate relief from those intrusive thoughts of "I can't do this" or "Why on earth did I say yes to this?" or my biggest nemesis, "You're not good enough; no one will like you."

Numerous studies have shown the stress-suppressing effects of particular scents, all of which appear on this list, plus a few bonus ones I love:

Peppermint, *Mentha piperita*

Thyme, *Thymus vulgaris*

Wintergreen, *Gaultheria fragrantissima*

Eucalyptus, *Eucalyptus globulus*

White camphor, *Cinnamomum camphora*

Cypress, *Cupressus sempervirens*

Lavender, *Lavandula angustifolia*

Tea Tree, *Melaleuca alternifolia*

Clary Sage, *Salvia sclarea*

Or, if in a true pinch, I just grab some Vicks VapoRub!

yourself out of a tailspin, just choose the one that best fits how you're feeling in the moment. Pigeonholing, or forcing your feelings into one of these two categories, can help diffuse the energy of a moment by creating some much-needed distance from your emotions.

In the identify step, you throw your word from the Fear Wheel into either the fear-of-not-being-good-enough bucket or the fear-of-not-being-in-control bucket. You could certainly attach more than one of your Fear Wheel words to what you're feeling in the moment, but the power is in choosing just one. This way, you can solidify your nebulous feeling into something you can grasp and hold.

The not-being-good-enough bucket

The fear of not being enough is rooted in how we feel about our own inadequacy or lack of worth. It stems from an underlying sense that we're not good enough, capable enough, or worthy of love or acceptance. This causes us to doubt ourselves, leading to feelings of insecurity and self-doubt. It can manifest in various ways, including feelings of inferiority, lack of self-confidence, low self-esteem, and anxiety around social situations.

The fear of not being good enough often is rooted in childhood experiences such as parental invalidation and rejection or other harsh criticisms and punishments during formative years. It can also come from family expectations, society's standards, comparison with others, and our own self-criticism. This can have a powerful effect on our lives—from undermining our confidence in social situations to creating anxieties about our future prospects.

The losing-control bucket

We all naturally desire to control ourselves, our environment, and our circumstances. When we feel like things are out of our hands or that life is happening *to* us instead of *for* us, it creates a sense of vulnerability and uncertainty that can be very frightening. And when faced with that uncertainty along with the possibility of danger, we become concerned and defensive, so our instinct is to take charge and attempt to control the situation.

This need for control is a basic human survival mechanism—it's our way of dealing with dangerous or unpredictable places or situations. However, when left unchecked the instinct to constantly see danger everywhere can make our world incredibly small while we hyper-focus on what might happen.

When we worry about making a wrong decision or face an unexpected change, or deal with other people's opinions and behaviors, we tend to avoid not only risks but also opportunities. We miss out on valuable moments in the present.

STEP 4: NAVIGATE (THE "MOVE THROUGH IT" STAGE)

The fourth step of the RAIN method is to navigate through your fear so you can move beyond it. Steps 1 through 3 of the RAIN method take place in the cognitive domain, but the final step is all about action! In this step, I recommend using a technique called box breathing to get through a fear episode. However, this is but one technique—you can also substitute any of your favorite neurohacks that appear in the next few chapters.

Thinking inside the box (box breathing)

Hearing the words "calm down" or "you just need to breathe" rarely has the intended effect for me. In fact, when they're directed at me, my typical response is to shoot back, "I *am* calm!" and "I *am* breathing!"

However, when used correctly, breathwork can be an incredibly powerful tool. There are many different breathwork techniques out there, some more complicated than others, but all aim to bring calm, mental clarity, and focus to the practitioner. My favorite of these techniques, box breathing, is a favorite of the US Navy SEALS. It's also the easiest technique to remember since, like a box's four sides, box breathing has just four simple steps.

Here's how to box breathe:

1. Slowly inhale to a count of four, filling your abdomen and lungs with air.

2. Hold that inhaled breath for a count of four.

3. Breathe out for a count of four.

4. Hold that exhale for a count of four.

Once you make box breathing a natural go-to, you can add a mantra to repeat between counts of four. I personally use "I am safe" to signal to my amygdala that all is well.

Then just repeat it until you feel more in control.

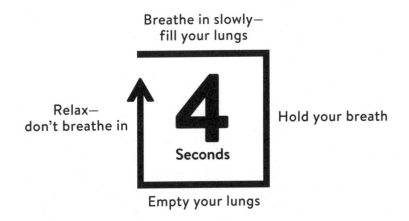

Breathe in slowly—
fill your lungs

Relax—
don't breathe in

4
Seconds

Hold your breath

Empty your lungs

APPLYING THE RAIN METHOD IN EVERYDAY LIFE

By investing energy into understanding, exploring, and navigating through your fears with tools like the RAIN method, you can begin to make peace and move beyond them.

The RAIN method can help you become more aware of your triggers and address them in the moment. Here are some tips for implementing this method for sustained success:

- Regularly check in with yourself throughout the day. Notice any tension in your body or thoughts that might indicate a fear response. Once you know your physical tells, see if you can get quicker at noticing them.

- Name your fears out loud, so they don't remain hiding in the shadows.

- Ask yourself questions about what you are afraid of and why.

- Practice self-compassion (this one is very hard for me, especially when my perfectionist tendencies take over!).

- Create a physical or digital reminder to implement the RAIN method whenever you start to enter a fear-arousal state.

Fear is natural, but it doesn't have to be overwhelming or incapacitating. The RAIN method provides a powerful framework for understanding and managing it, so don't be afraid to give it a shot! If it's not your cup of tea don't worry, there are more neurohack options in the coming chapters.

Living courageously means being willing to move through fear rather than avoiding or denying its presence in your life.

Living courageously means being willing to move through fear rather than avoiding or denying its presence in your life. By using the RAIN method, you can better understand the sources of your fears and then use that understanding to take meaningful action to overcome them.

THE RAIN METHOD IN ACTION

One of the first times I used the RAIN method was, naturally, during a cyclone in the Adriatic Sea in Croatia.

A month after my mom died, one of my best friends, Elaine, invited me to accompany her and her boyfriend, Eric, on a boat tour of Croatia during a popular event called Yacht Week. We booked spots on a ten-person, forty-foot sailboat that only allowed for about four square feet of personal space per person.

Upon reaching the docked boat, we were greeted by a surly man swigging from a bottle of clear plum brandy who introduced himself as Janko, our captain. Elaine, Eric, and I all exchanged a glance that said, "This is how we die."

Janko told us to stow our luggage in the hull and pointed to where we would sleep. Since Elaine and Eric were a couple, they obviously would sleep in the same berth. Captain Janko pointed to a twin bed in a coffin and said, "That's yours. Your roommate should be showing up shortly."

Wait. What? The bed was literally a twin mattress in a drawer. You had to crawl in, and if you sat up too quickly, you might give yourself a concussion. Where was my "roommate" going to sleep? With my American sense of personal space in alarm mode, I began to panic.

"It's fine . . . it's fine . . . it's going to be fine," I told myself. "You've spent more than a few nights sharing a bed with a stranger you just met—this will be no different . . . just with less sexy time." Luckily, it was just fine. The woman who would become my bunkmate was more focused on staying out all night and doing the swim of shame back to the boat with her friends each morning.

For the first four days, the skies were blue and the ocean water bluer, which was a balm to my tattered emotions as I struggled with both the grief of losing my mother and the elation of being free of her round-the-clock care. I spent most days on the bow of our boat in contemplation or reading, letting the salty sea heal my wounds.

On the fourth day, which broke with another robin's-egg-blue sky, Elaine and I went ashore to the island of Vis. Until then, we had docked either on or very close to an island. However, this particular island was filled to bursting with boats and tourists, so we dropped anchor in a little cove and took a twenty-minute water taxi ride to shore. After a full day exploring the picturesque village, we stopped in a cafe serving local seafood. The sun was setting on the hot day as we took the last bites of our squid-ink pasta.

Suddenly, the heavens opened up. People screamed and ran for shelter from the torrential downpour. Elaine, a native Scot, and I, a former field biologist, simply looked at each other—shrugged—and held our plastic menus over our heads until our waitress came to cash out our bill. We were confident the deluge would soon stop.

We were wrong.

Wine was the price of indoor refuge at the next cafe, but when we found ourselves on glass-number-I-don't-know we needed to make a decision. With a raised eyebrow to convey she didn't think this was a quick downpour, Elaine said brightly, "Well, let's see how things are looking outside!"

I was the first to step out of the cafe and found my legs submerged to the calf on what had been a dry street just an hour before. We were in trouble.

We flew down to the docks and were told that no boats were leaving until the next morning.

"Okay, not ideal, but not the end of the world," Elaine declared in her Scottish brogue. "We can grab a hotel room for the night and then head back to the boat in the morning." Perfect! But as we would soon learn, all lodgings on the island had been long sold out for Yacht Week.

Water was cascading from the sky in sheets, and with no place else to go, wine it was! We found another bar.

But the bars would eventually close, and we knew no one but each other on this tiny island. I was trying to resign myself to spending the night huddled together on a flooded street in the town square. I was in full fear mode. I had never spent a night unsheltered, much less during a cyclone! As my mind went offline, Elaine's went into action.

She slapped her hands on the bar, paid our bill, and shooed us out into the underwater streets. The solution to our problem came in the form of a bright, shiny banana bobbing in the harbor. Yes, a banana. An inflatable one used for joy rides—certainly not intended for rescue missions involving a trip into the Adriatic . . . at night . . . during a cyclone.

But we had to try.

We walked down to the dock to beg, borrow, or steal a ride home, though let's be real—stealing a boat would have meant certain death since neither of us knew how to drive a speedboat, let alone a banana-toting one. After some negotiation and an exorbitant amount of untraceable cash, we were able to convince someone to pull us on the inflatable banana pulled by a two-seater speedboat to the relative safety of Captain Janko and our boat. We laughed maniacally during the entire twenty-minute ride, convinced that this was either the best or worst idea we'd ever had.

You are reading this book, so clearly I made it off the banana and onto the boat alive. But my experience is the perfect one to talk about how I applied the RAIN method to go from a fear-frozen mess to a banana-boat-riding maven.

Step 1: Recognize (the "Feel It" stage)

First, this was not a nuanced experience. My fear score was super high! My shoulders looked like I was in a constant shrug, my teeth were sore from clenching my jaw, and my heart was pounding a mile a minute. But I knew my tells and could easily recognize that I was letting my fear of not having control of the situation run away with me and compromise my problem-solving ability.

Step 2: Assign (the "Name It" stage)

Standing on the docks, I was absolutely dreading an unknown future and my ability to navigate it—"dread" being my easy-to-choose Fear Wheel word here.

Step 3: Identify (the "Sort It" stage)

We often struggle to choose between the fear of not being enough and the fear of not being in control. But the choice this time was not a struggle for me! This was 100 percent the fear of not being in control. I chose the devil I knew (getting to the boat) versus the devil I didn't (sleeping rough in a foreign country during a cyclone).

Was it the best or safest option? Probably not. Do I regret it? Absolutely not!

Step 4: Navigate (the "Move Through It" stage)

I needed to get on that crazy floating banana. In hindsight, it was vastly more dangerous than sleeping in a wet gutter, but at the time my mind gravitated toward safety like a lighthouse in a storm. And safety on that night meant being in my tiny, borrowed coffin bed. Danger was staying on an island with no safe harbor.

The banana boat also felt good because it was action. Resigning myself to gutter sleeping felt like giving up, like a dangerous defeat. So, using my RAIN method and box breathing for all I was worth, I hiked up my dress and straddled the inflatable banana to be pulled by the tiny two-seater speedboat, holding on to the handle for dear life as we took off into the storm. After twenty minutes of banana riding in the pelting rain and wind so loud we could barely hear our own voices, we arrived at our boat, soaked but safe and mildly hysterical.

Captain Janko, who never left the boat, said he had not seen anyone either so stupid or so brave in a very long time. I chose to

How to Slow Brain Aging

As we age, our brains tend to lose some of their plasticity. However, by engaging in activities that stimulate the formation of new neural networks, we can slow down this process and even reverse it in some cases. Not only can learning new skills help preserve cognitive functions like memory, but they can also increase creativity and problem-solving capabilities, as well as reduce stress levels. Feeding your brain a constant diet of curiosity, creativity, education, and new and novel experiences will help stave off the deleterious effects of aging.

Just as our muscles atrophy with lack of use and strengthen with proper diet and exercise, so do our brains. Neuroplasticity is our brain's way of adapting and learning from new situations by forming and reorganizing its connections in response to new experiences or changes in our environment.

When we change how we think, what we do, and how we behave, our brains change, too.

take that as a compliment since, in my experience, the best stories are born from being a little of both.

Neuroplasticity: How Your Brain Grows and Changes

Imagine you're a bird soaring above a large city. Looking down, you see wide roads filled with multiple lanes of traffic, smaller single-lane roads, and pathways so narrow that no cars can fit on them. This bird's-eye view of a city is similar to the way the neural pathways are arranged in your brain. Every time you do, think, or feel something, you're using one of these roads in your brain known as neural pathways.

The more you do, think, or feel a particular thing, the wider and better paved the road becomes. The less that road is used by not feeling, thinking, or doing a particular thing, the less space it takes up in your neural "city." Habitual things like brushing your teeth are well-traveled freeways, and something you're doing for the very first time is a tiny footpath in the woods.

Neuroplasticity is a process by which our brains can adapt to changes in our internal or external environment. This umbrella term encompasses how our nervous system can grow, modify, and reorganize itself to adapt to an ever-changing world. Where "neuro" is meant to signify neurons, the specialized cells of the brain and nervous system, the use of the term "plasticity" is rooted in its definition as something malleable. Scientists once believed that our ability to grow new neurons ceased after birth, but recent research has shown that because of neuroplasticity, we can create new neural connections, adjust neural pathways, and, in some cases, even create brand-new neurons regardless of age.

No matter our age, we can change how our brains are wired with the right tools and actions.

As we have gained a deeper understanding of neuroplasticity, we have discovered that you can—and should—teach an old dog new tricks! From the creation of new neurons to the growth of new connections, neuroplasticity is an essential piece of the fear/courage paradox we discussed in Chapter 3. No matter our age, we can change

Bravery Break: How to Use Repetition to Train Your Brain to Be Brave

Here is a simple yet powerful way to start sending your amygdala to the gym:

1. **Identify your fear:** Write it down, say it out loud, make it tangible.

2. **Devise a plan:** Decide how you can safely expose yourself to this fear, little by little. Again, if you are looking to address a fear that is deeply rooted in trauma, please have professional support to guide you—no need to have a lifetime fear of snakes and decide to jump into a pit that would make Indiana Jones run for the exit.

3. **Baby steps:** Start with small doses of your fear, then gradually increase your exposure as you grow more comfortable.

4. **Reflect and repeat:** After each exposure, take some time to reflect on the experience and then repeat the process until the fear becomes manageable.

The more frequently you expose yourself to the things you're afraid of in a way that best works for you, the less power those triggers will hold. It's a gradual process, but with time, repetition can help you transform those fears into just another aspect of your daily life.

Desensitization allows you to dismantle your fears one piece at a time, transforming them from towering walls into stepping stones on your journey to a more courageous mind.

how our brains are wired with the right tools and actions. We can turn those unhelpful highways into overgrown jungle footpaths and build new roads that align us with who we want to be, instead of who we are now.

When we experience a fear trigger paired with the same response enough times, our brain creates a sort of "default" setting that it will use for all similar future experiences. There is no exact rule for how many times it takes for this to happen, which is why it's essential to examine major fear-inducing events you experience, so you don't create a freeway for them.

PUTTING YOUR BEST FOOT FORWARD

One of my earliest memories was riding a full-grown quarter horse, standing about four and a half feet off the ground, with my Auntie Myrtle holding me in place. Now, Auntie Myrtle was not an auntie directly related to me, but she was one of my tribal community aunties who shared the work of raising me. Connecting me to my Indigenous paternal heritage, though I would never meet that particular man in the flesh, Myrtle felt it essential that horses be a central aspect of my young life.

Although I began riding at age three, I wasn't expected to care for the horses until I got older. By age seven, I was mucking stalls, polishing tack, and cleaning hooves. It was during a routine hoof cleaning that I had one of the biggest scares of my young life to that point, one that could've created a neural pathway I would've struggled with for the rest of my life.

My eighth birthday had just passed, and Auntie Myrtle and I had just come back from a ride. Hamilton, a feisty Appaloosa with a dark spotted coat, was already groomed and in his stall munching hay as we were both getting my horse, Cinnamon, ready to do the same. Cinnamon, a very lazy brown quarter horse, was mine to ride because he was the definition of chill.

So you can imagine my shock when Cinnamon stepped right on top of my foot that day.

Events that have strong emotions associated with them create instant superhighways of memory, so I can still recall everything about that moment. I had just cleaned his back left hoof and was about to do the right one when I broke one of the cardinal rules of horsemanship: Always have a hand on the horse's rump if you plan to be back there doing anything. As I went to leave the left hoof and go to the right, I removed my hands. Cinnamon, who was distracted by seeing his beloved hay being forked into his stall, probably didn't realize I was still back there. So he repositioned his right back hoof on top of my small, eight-year-old foot, covering it from toe to ankle. Luckily, he didn't put much weight on the move.

I knew that if I yelled or screamed, Cinnamon would panic and crush my foot under him. Thanks to my experience with horses, I was able to maintain calm even though I was terrified. In an even voice I said, "Auntie Myrtle, please get this horse off my foot." She looked down in horror, grabbed the bridle, and gently moved Cinnamon forward.

Once Cinnamon was off my foot and at a safe distance, I collapsed in tears. Pulling my shoe off, I found a hoof-shaped print that would turn into a bruise, but nothing was broken. After Auntie Myrtle palpated around the bones and found that I had no problem standing or walking, she said, "Alright, get up, we're going back out on a ride." With my lower jaw somewhere around my belly button and my eyes wide, I said, "What? No. I don't want to. I just got stepped on!"

Auntie Myrtle, with her salt-and-pepper mane, which went from black to gray when she was just a teen, of untamable curls framing a look that brooked no argument, responded, "Exactly. This is why you need to get back on that horse right now. Otherwise, you may never ride again. Not because you couldn't, but because you will be too afraid to.

"So, get up, and let's go."

And go we did.

If we hadn't, it could have taken just that one time for me to have a lifetime of fear around horses. But instead, I love riding to this day because Auntie Myrtle didn't let that fear take root and grow. Although I haven't had regular access to horses as an adult, any chance I get to ride, I jump on with both feet (well, one foot and then the other). The joy of riding may have been taken away from me that day had my Auntie Myrtle not insisted that I create a quick new experiential memory to associate with Cinnamon to replace the terrified one I had when I thought I would lose my foot.

FACING YOUR FEARS: DESENSITIZATION AND REPETITION

"I know kung fu."

Perhaps the most jealous-worthy part of the first *Matrix* film was when Keanu Reeves's character, Neo, was able to instantly upload knowledge and skill. Alas, such instant gratification is still in the realm of science fiction, so we mere mortals must learn things the hard way through practice. Writing, cooking, and sports all need dedication and time spent being mediocre or even terrible before you can get to being good. Desensitization, in essence, is a process where our mind becomes less responsive to a stressor after repeated exposure, where we practice in a low-risk way to train our brain to be less reactive to a particular trigger.

Desensitization, in essence, is a process where our mind becomes less responsive to a stressor after repeated exposure, where we practice in a low-risk way to train our brain to be less reactive to a particular trigger.

When you engage in activities that challenge the thoughts you have in response to a fear-inducing trigger, new courageous pathways are formed in your brain. Over time, these courageous pathways will become stronger as they are reinforced through repetition, which will help weaken and eventually replace your old fear responses.

Desensitization is not about suppressing your fears but rather about confronting them in a safe, controlled way. Every time you face a stressful situation and survive, your brain records it as a win in your favor. With enough repetitions, your brain begins to realize that the outcome is not as catastrophic as it initially perceived. This helps gradually reduce your fear response.

Before I began writing professionally, I was terrified of getting negative feedback. Logically, I knew that feedback and iteration are essential to creating good outcomes, but emotionally I dreaded any and all criticism of my writing. I dealt so poorly with my first round of professional feedback that I hid from the file and the email for an entire week before I was ready to get back to it. Now, after many rounds of try/fail/repeat, I can welcome feedback from trusted sources with more openness and less terror.

Desensitization aims to confront what triggers your fearful response without experiencing any actual danger or harm. Desensitization and exposure therapy are commonly used interchangeably, though most would say that desensitization is what people do on their own for the more low-grade fears of life. Exposure therapy is what you do with a clinical psychologist for the trauma-induced terrors that benefit from professional support. At the heart of both is practice makes perfect (or close enough to perfect, since none of us are perfectionists anymore, right?).

When we practice exposing ourselves to a low-risk fear trigger, we can begin to train our brain, through the power of neuroplasticity, to understand that the thing we're irrationally scared of isn't so bad after all. More new information and new experiences result in your brain forming new connections and pathways to help you survive an ever-changing world.

RAINing My Way Out of the Pandemic

There are seasons when we're zooming at top speed through the marathons of our life. We feel strong and in tip-top shape. In other seasons, we're huffing and puffing as we struggle to even cross the one-mile mark. Both are valid, and neither are permanent.

Since I've been banging on about courage being fluid like our skeletal muscles, with times of peak strength and times of floppy weakness, I want to share how my extroverted self had to rebuild the "being around humans again" muscle after the COVID-19 pandemic.

I spent the pandemic in Southern California, where Los Angeles took lockdown very seriously. When it was finally time for us to emerge from our sourdough bread caves, I found I sort of forgot how to be a social human in a room full of new people. Before lockdown, I had a consistently chaotic travel schedule where I was meeting, chatting, laughing, and crying with new humans constantly. It was my norm.

Then my world shrank down to the size of my laptop screen.

In my mind, I thought the end of the pandemic would be like the World War II photograph of the now famous kissing couple in Times Square as they celebrated the end of the war. Or simply that there would be this definitive end and we would all celebrate in the streets and return to normal. As you know, that wasn't the case.

During that slow-burn return, I found myself quite anxious at the prospect of chatting and laughing or really even meeting new humans. I had been in hypervigilance for so long, on constant high alert for anyone not in my bubble getting too close, that my courage-to-meet-new-people muscle had gone soft (like my glutes, but that's another discussion entirely).

My first big on-stage post-pandemic speaking event was terrifying.

Two hours to showtime, I get a call from the client who hired me that tragedy had struck. The night before, just outside where I was to speak, a man was killed when a tree toppled during a violent storm. After I conveyed my shock and sympathies for the community's loss, she assured me that the show would go on, but that I should be prepared for some of the attendees to have known the man.

My mind spiraled with infinite scenarios, most of which included me delivering a terrible show and making an utter arse of myself.

Enter stage left: The RAIN method for the win. Recognize . . . Assign . . . Identify . . . Navigate

Thirty minutes to showtime. Tech check is going a bit sideways, but we're improvising. This is pretty normal for live shows of this size, so I'm not too worried.

I start using all the strong scents to distract my amygdala

Fifteen minutes to showtime, the turnout is so large that venue staff are pulling out more seating to accommodate. But I didn't know they had the possibility of expanding capacity and so didn't have enough physical materials that I normally use in my events for everyone. This was when I really started to feel the weakness of my talking-to-new-humans muscle. All the attendees were so lovely and interested and chatty. I worried I might need a nap before going onstage to recharge from exuding all this energy just chatting with them!

I was massaging my HeGu Valley for all I was worth.

Five minutes to showtime, Michelle, whom you met in previous chapters, serving dual roles as bestie and my personal event manager, comes running into the greenroom shouting, "Give me your spare shoes!"

"What?!" I asked. Michelle, frantic as she has been setting up the remaining materials for each guest and doing some crowd control, flaps her right hand with the "gimmie-gimmie" gesture while her left is waving around a pair of three-inch heels that have miraculously both had their soles come off at the same time in the same way, making them completely useless for walking. Luckily, given my history of spraining my ankles in all sorts of random ways, I have a pair of flats I wear to and from shows and a pair of on-stage stunners that are for stage only. Michelle grabs the flats and runs back out to finish prep before we go live.

T minus two minutes.

At this point, I figure the only place that I can take a moment to center myself before going onstage is the ladies loo. I escape to the silent solace of the single bathroom and take my remaining sixty seconds to box breathe as if my life depended on it.

I continue my box breathing as my heels clatter on the tile backstage. Introductions are made and I walk onstage. Then, you know what happens?

I proceed to have one of the best shows of my career.

Seconds into the show and all throughout our two hours together, as I looked across the hundreds of people who chose to share their time and energy with me, I remembered why I used to keep my talking-to-new-humans muscle in top shape. The vibrant energy, exuberance, and vitality of others enjoying themselves—connecting to new best friends, laughing with abandon—reminded me why this is what I do. Because I love the feeling of aliveness of hundreds of people gathered together by choice to launch into the abyss of fear and courage.

Building, or rebuilding, your courage muscles doesn't need to be hard or lengthy. But practicing and exposing yourself to scary things that will ultimately bring you value will result in your getting better at them, making them less scary each and every time.

Whether it's a fear response or a courageous act, practice makes (almost) perfect.

CHAPTER 9

The Biological Keys to Courage

Jump off the cliff and build your
wings on the way down.
—RAY BRADBURY

I've called California home for most of my life, its soaring peaks and deep lowland valleys a constant backdrop to my existence. From my doorstep, I've gazed upon the San Gabriel, the Diablo, and the Santa Cruz mountain ranges. I suppose it's no surprise then that I see life similarly, as a series of high peaks and low valleys. Inevitably, there are times when you feel on top, powerful, like you're winning at life. As if you can see for miles and nothing can touch you.

Then, of course, there are times when you're in the trough of the valley, at your lowest point, when it seems like everything is rushing down toward you unabated. When all you can do is look up and feel that the climb is too steep, the peaks on which you were just dancing are suddenly too far away. And that you may never dance on them again.

Living courageously doesn't mean that you never dwell in the valley. Rather, it's about exploring the entire state of your human experience, including the highest peaks, the lowest valleys, and everything in between.

One of the most intriguing qualities of humanity is our ability to show tenacity in the face of adversity. Whether you're seeking new relationships, a career pivot, or physical feats of daring, this chapter will give you some cheat codes to try next time you feel like you could use a bravery boost. In this chapter you'll find neurohacks that act more on your physical body rather than those that enhance your psychological experience (which appear in the next chapter). The difference between the two lies within the approach you take to influence how you experience fear and courage in the moment.

The biological neurohacks found in this chapter involve ways to physically trick your fear-arousal system to return to a sense of calm using things like touch, sound, and smell. From vagal nerve stimulation to binaural beats, there is an array of tools and techniques that target the biology underlying fear and courage so you can take action even when your chest starts to tighten and your jaw begins to clench.

I have personally tried each of the neurohacking techniques described in this chapter (and the book as a whole!) during both my peak and valley seasons. Not every one will be the best fit for your unique set of experiences or preferences, so look at what follows as a buffet for you to sample and find what works best for you.

The Courage Equation

Taking action is the key to living a courageous life. According to research, those who take action—no matter how small—tend to feel more courageous and less fearful than those who don't act at all. This of course makes sense, given that acting on our goals helps us build confidence in our abilities, which can help us feel more secure and less scared. Whether physical or mental, any intentional forward movement will help break fear's hold on you.

My personal courage equation is:

Fear + Action = Courage

Although there's a lot of talk of fight or flight around fear, we're much more likely to sit and stew. With fictional fear-based threats, your body still wants to enter battle mode to protect you, but it is entirely unnecessary. Instead, your fear response turns inward. You ruminate over doubts and insecurities, digging yourself deeper into a hole of distress that's entirely of your own making. And then you still have to wrestle with some of the side effects of fear: sweaty palms, digestive upset, racing heart. The more time you spend living in that fear, stewing in it, ruminating over it, the more afraid of the world you become.

In most modern societies, we simply can't escape our fears and problems by either running from them or fighting them. But movement helps when it comes to calming a frightened body—by dissipating the feelings of fear with action.

Fear + Action = Courage

Whether it's something unseen like the RAIN method (see Chapter 8), or something else that requires more physical exertion, action helps calm your amygdala and quench its thirst for action. *Fear + Action = Courage* When your fear state is aroused, your amygdala *wants* you to do something. This is where the neurohacks come in—they will help calm your amygdala so that you can approach life's complex challenges with logic instead of panic.

Living bravely is not just a mental exercise—it's a neurobiological one.

The good news is that we know we have more control over our brains than previously thought (thanks, science!). We can use the neurohacks to rewire our brains to respond differently in stressful situations. Studies have shown that regular practice of these techniques can help reduce stress levels in the moment and overall over time. By de-escalating our fear responses to the daily psychosocial pressures of our lives, these tools allow us to approach life with more courage and confidence.

The Power of Touch

Touch can be a powerful tool for reducing fear and increasing courage. Whether it's a hug from someone you actually want to hug you, a furry cuddle from a beloved pet, or something more unique like the neurohacks in this section, touch has been scientifically proven to de-escalate our fear response. Welcomed touch increases the levels of our "happy brain chemicals"—oxytocin, dopamine, and serotonin—while decreasing the levels of our stress hormones, such as norepinephrine and cortisol, resulting in increased feelings of relaxation and, thus, safety.

We are biologically wired to crave physical contact, so why not use this natural inclination to help ourselves feel braver?

VAGUS NERVE STIMULATION

Vagus nerve stimulation brings a sense of calm to our bodies by targeting the longest and most complex of our cranial nerves. The vagus nerve starts in the brain and extends all the way to the abdomen; it becomes activated when our brains are analyzing if we're safe or in danger. While the vagus nerve has many functions, some of its most important roles are regulating emotions and the "rest-and-digest" parasympathetic nervous system that's in charge when we feel safe. Vagus nerve stimulation has been shown to decrease anxiety, stress, depression, and in some cases even improve the symptoms of post-traumatic stress disorder (PTSD).

By reducing heart rate and blood pressure and calming breathing, vagus nerve stimulation promotes relaxation, positive emotions, and a sense of well-being. This can be an especially important tool to have in your toolbox when you need to de-escalate or rebound from a fear-arousal response. You can get your vagus nerve stimulated in a doctor's office with a specialized machine, but there are many other ways to do it without specialized equipment or training. In addition to the HeGu Meridian massage (see page 15), here are some of my favorites!

Vagal massage

Vagus nerve massage involves applying moderate pressure in circular or stroking motions to muscles in the neck, ears, and tops of the shoulders. Specific targets include the trapezius and sternocleidomastoid muscles. The former are located at the tops of the shoulders and are used to move the head, neck, and shoulder blades. The latter can be found along the sides of the neck (which get engaged when rotating the head) and at the back of the neck, extending from the base of the skull.

Since the vagus nerve starts in the brain and runs down through your chest and abdomen, your neck and head are the easiest places to stimulate it with massage. A word to keep in mind for this: nourishing. Even if you like deep-tissue massages, the goal here is to simply stimulate the area, so be sure to go easy on the pressure. It may be helpful to add lotion or oil so that your hands can easily slide over your skin—but this isn't a requirement since I want you to be able to do this for yourself in the car, in a meeting, or on a bathroom break.

The MacEwen Triangle

Place your index finger just behind your earlobe, but before you get to your hairline, in a thumb-size spot of your skull called the MacEwen or suprameatal triangle or, more simply, "the triangle." Gently massage this area for about two minutes using circular motions with medium pressure. Then, move farther down along the neck toward the base of the skull and lightly press on either side of the spine with both hands for another minute or so while breathing deeply and slowly.

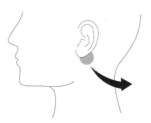

Collarbone and Neck

Start by finding an area along your collarbone that feels tender when gently pressed. Take a few deep breaths to relax each tender spot. Then, place both hands around the back of your neck and use gentle circular motions to massage the muscles on either side of your spine. As you work on each muscle group, focus on releasing any tension or tightness that may be present in the area. You can also use kneading motions on either side of the muscle groups if desired. Continue this for several minutes until you feel relief from tension in those areas.

Freezing out fear

I saved this vagus nerve stimulation method for last because I hate being cold. However, holding your breath and splashing very cold water on your face, taking a cold shower, jumping into a cold ocean for a swim or doing a full-body ice bath are all ways to stimulate your vagus nerve. Currently, there are no medical recommendations for how cold or how long is ideal—as long as you hold your breath while at least briefly submerging your nose and mouth, you'll reap the benefits. This neurohack is part of our dive reflex, a complex physiologic reaction thought to have evolved as a way for mammals to conserve oxygen, slow down the heart rate (and thus the workload on the heart), and protect vital organs while being submerged in water.

And while I recommend a cold ocean swim, this isn't always a practical option. Simply submerging your face in any cold water is a quick and easy way to stimulate the vagus nerve and help bring more calm into your day.

FLOAT THERAPY

If the idea of floating in a dark, soundproof tank sends shivers down your spine, consider this: There are many different types of float tanks, and research is now supporting their value for decreasing anxiety and strengthening a sense of calm that lasts long after your session.

Specifically, research has found that Floatation-REST (Reduced Environmental Stimulation Therapy) can positively impact everyone, but especially those suffering from extreme types of clinical anxiety. As is the case with most human-based research, the positive effects were not seen by all participants, but many reported feeling more relaxed, less stressed, and less tense after a session. As the value of float therapy becomes more widely known, public float tank locations are beginning to pop up in many cities beyond their original sites of Los Angeles and New York.

STIMMING

Do you chew on your pen? Or sigh loudly when frustrated? Stimming, or self-stimulation, is loosely defined as any repetitive body movement or sound. Although stimming was initially associated with the behavior of neurodiverse individuals, such as those on the autism spectrum, most of us exhibit stims of some kind.

Occasionally, uncontrollable stimming can become disruptive to daily living. However, in most cases we repeat a stim because the action feels good to us. It can soothe us, help us feel calmer, and increase our focus, making it a powerful tool to utilize, and certainly not something to hide or be ashamed of. Common types of stimming include whistling, foot tapping, drumming of fingers, hair twirling, humming, nail-biting, and knuckle cracking.

Stims, colloquially referred to as nervous habits, may even help us better detect a strong emotion just below the surface, such as tapping your foot when anxiously waiting for something or someone. Your personal stims often become more pronounced or frequent as you become increasingly stressed, afraid, or agitated.

Stims can also vary in frequency, which is often also connected to our emotions. How often stimming occurs differs from person to person. For example, you may only tap your pencil when you're anxious or impatient. For me, my thumb cuticles reveal my stress level. My stim is to use my index finger to worry-rub at the side of my thumb; I have done it for so long that I have little ripply ridges permanently shaped into my thumbnails! But I find it releases some of the nervous energy I have when I'm under stress, especially if there's no other way for me to physically release that energy. After years of letting my cuticles take the brunt of my stress, I now wear a fidget ring each and every day.

By focusing your attention on something benign, like spinning a tiny ball bearing around on a ring, you can help yourself not focus quite so much on a stress trigger.

By focusing your attention on something benign, like spinning a tiny ball bearing around on a ring, you can help yourself not focus quite so much on a stress trigger.

In addition to fidget rings, there are many other options on the market, such as Calm Strips (adhesive strips of textured fabric that can be scratched, stroked, or rubbed whenever you feel anxious or stressed), kinetic fidgeters (objects you can use for repetitive behavior, such as fidget spinners or fidget toys), and stress balls. Though none of these have been rigorously studied to support the how and why they work, given their low cost and low risk, I've found many adults benefit from them during stressful experiences.

The Air We Breathe

Breathwork is incredibly powerful, deceptively simple, and easy to do. Paradoxically, it can also be very difficult (well, at least for me). Breathwork is an effective way to reduce stress and cultivate courage in your life, though for many of us, focusing on our breath is an incredibly difficult thing to do in the moment. But it is something I persist in trying, despite multiple failures, because I know the power of our breath to activate our parasympathetic nervous system (PNS) and help regulate our stress response.

I like to use the term "breathwork" instead of "breathing" to reinforce the distinction between the two: Breathing is what we do automatically without thinking; breathwork is when we actively bring our prefrontal cortex into the game and consciously control how we breathe or when we hold our breath.

By using intentional breathing patterns, breathwork both increases oxygen levels in our bodies and activates our "rest-and-digest" parasympathetic nervous system to return a sense of calm to our bodies and minds.

Breathwork also has additional physical benefits such as reducing blood pressure levels, improving respiration rates, reducing fatigue levels (due to increased oxygen intake), and relieving stress-induced aches, such as headaches or back pain. Mentally, intentional breathwork can do so many things that a list is more appropriate.

Intentional breathwork can:

- Help reduce anxiety levels by calming your nervous system
- Increase focus by improving your concentration skills
- Improve sleep quality by allowing you to fall asleep faster
- Improve your cognitive functioning
- Boost your self-esteem
- Uplift your mood
- Provide emotional stability

The types of breathwork outlined below are by no means an exhaustive list. They're just my favorites because they're the simplest and easiest to remember in the moments when I need them most.

COURAGE QUEST: Who's Your Dive Buddy?

While scuba diving off the coast of the Isla Mujeres in the sparkling cerulean waters of the Mexican Caribbean, I almost succumbed to the "rapture of the deep." Officially known as nitrogen narcosis, it results in a euphoric state of impaired judgment and coordination akin to being almost instantly drunk. Just like the alcoholic version of liquid courage, nitrogen narcosis gives you a false sense of invincibility as your fear of dying floats away on the current.

Of course, reaching this state is meant to be avoided, but I'm easily distracted and it almost cost me my life.

Craig and I were diving a reef wall, a near-vertical massive outgrowth of hard coral that tends to go down too deep for recreational divers and often faces an expansive open ocean. These complex structures are bursting with colorful life including fish, sponges, urchins, anemones, and other visually alluring sea creatures. Although we were already around eighty feet deep, the reef wall stretched hundreds of feet into the blue abyss, well beyond what I could see. Due to the complete lack of any visual indicators like a seabed, I should have been paying close attention to my depth gauge. But I was so enthralled with the experience that depth checking was the last thing on my mind.

As I rode the gentle current basking in the breathtaking beauty in front of me, I felt an overwhelming peace and tranquility. At the time, I thought it was just the exquisiteness of the wall, when in fact it was nitrogen narcosis setting in.

Luckily, I had a dive buddy!

Craig, serving as my wingman, helped me survive my underwater peril. Or, in this case, saved me from my own choices.

Lost in the quick onset of fluffy happy rainbow sensations, I didn't respond to Craig banging on his air tank, a standard way to get someone's attention underwater. When that didn't work, he descended, grabbed me by the vest, and with terror-stricken eyes pointed to my depth gauge. I had accidentally descended to 127 feet. (Nitrogen narcosis begins to become debilitating at 110 feet.)

So, who is your dive buddy? Someone who would, or has, saved you from descending into the murky depths? Describing your ideal dive buddy helps articulate your needs and desires to strengthen existing relationships and cultivate new ones that can support your journey to a more courageous life.

Describe someone in your life, past or present, who has made you feel safe. How did trust develop between you two?

Describe someone in your life who always gave you courage (they can be the same as your safety human, but sometimes they are two different people). How did trust develop between you two?

How do you feel when you're with your dive buddy? Describe your thoughts, emotions, and even behaviors.

One small note: A common question I get during workshops when I reach the breathwork portion is, "Do I have to breathe through my nose?"

Many practices will say yes, but scientifically speaking the role our nostrils play in the benefits of active breath control is not yet fully understood (or has even been studied much). As someone who always seems to have a stuffy nose, nostril breathing isn't always available to me. However, my go-to advice is always: "If it works well for you, then do it!"

DIAPHRAGMATIC BREATHING (BELLY BREATHING)

Diaphragmatic breathing (also known as "abdominal breathing," "belly breathing," or "deep breathing") involves taking slow, deep breaths from the diaphragm—the muscle located between your chest cavity and abdomen. This type of breathing instantly stimulates the vagus nerve, resulting in beneficial physical and psychological effects such as lowering blood pressure, slowing a runaway heart-beat, and calming your fear-arousal response.

Here's how to do it:

1. Inhale slowly through your nose, allowing your stomach to expand outward as you do so.

2. Exhale slowly out of your mouth, pushing all the air out with each breath. As you exhale, concentrate on gently pulling the stomach back toward the spine, like you're trying to zip up a tight pair of jeans after getting them out of the dryer.

3. Repeat this process for ten to fifteen breaths, focusing on drawing deep and slow breaths from your diaphragm rather than shallow breaths from your chest.

UJJAYI BREATH (VICTORIOUS BREATH)

This type of breathwork is often used in yoga. It involves deep, audible breaths of equal duration, inhaling through your nose and exhaling out through your mouth while making a "haaahhh" sound from the back of your throat. Of all the breathwork examples I've shared here, this one makes me the most uncomfortable in public because I feel like a roaring, angry dragon when I do it, so instead I usually sound more like an angry mouse from embarrassment.

SILENT STRESS WHISTLES

A stress whistle is a long, skinny metal tube that looks like a dog whistle but makes no sound (for humans or dogs). Most are worn on a chain as a necklace, so they're always within reach. Because they're quite narrow, the whistle forces you to lengthen your exhalation as you aim to count to ten while breathing out. Slow exhales naturally cause your heart rate to decrease. While repeating the slow exhale, focus on releasing tension from your forehead, shoulders, and jaw. Having a stress whistle as a necklace helps provide a physical reminder to practice your breathwork and, as an added bonus, can be a fashion statement!

SPEAK IT OUT

If you find yourself stuck in a rumination cycle of worrying about the past or future, you can short-circuit your internal monologue by verbally and audibly speaking exactly what is swirling in your head, so it can release its hold on you. To do this, place your hands on your body in a way that brings comfort. Maybe it's wrapping them around your arms like you're cold. For me, I put a hand on my heart and one on my belly. The hand on my heart is to remind me I am loved, and the belly hand reminds me to breathe with my diaphragm and fill my belly with air.

With your hands in place, simply speak out loud exactly what you're focusing on. You can do this to a trusted human, a mirror, or even a pet. I'm alone a lot in my work, but I have my trusted super dog, Bandit, at my side nearly all the time, so I usually direct my verbalization his way. I often wonder if that makes him a therapist dog.

The Sounds of Our Lives

From ancient chants and classical music to singing songs of bravery and strength to repeating mantras that bring us serenity and peace, sound can profoundly affect our emotional state. Sound has long been known to be a powerful tool for calming the body and mind and can help us reframe our experience of fear and cultivate more courageous approaches in life. In this section, we'll explore some novel ways for you to add sound to your courage kit.

SOUND BATHS

Sound baths are therapeutic practices in which harmonies and frequencies produced by chimes, crystal bowls, and gongs help you relax and find peace. These immersive tones shift slowly to help you feel enveloped or "bathed" in vibrations. In a 2020 study that measured the relaxing effects of sound baths, people who spent forty minutes in one reported a marked reduction in fatigue, tension, and anger, with an increase in clarity and vigor.

It was a crisp Thursday evening when I attended my first sound bath session atop the Malibu bluffs overlooking the Pacific Ocean. I'd been hearing about sound baths for a few years, but never had the opportunity to experience one myself. I was nervous but also excited as questions ran through my head: "What is going to happen? Will people like me? Will I look ridiculous?" But I pushed through . . . for science!

With crashing Pacific waves as our backdrop, the group lay down on blankets and pillows and closed our eyes. The facilitator invited us to take deep belly breaths. As we all settled into this position, a wonderful thing happened: I could feel my fear subsiding! The gentle music was incredibly soothing until the two women behind me—who were clearly newbies and were downing two full bottles of chardonnay—giggled uncontrollably.

By the end of the session I felt lighter than air, as if I had been transported to another realm entirely. The people were so incredibly kind and welcoming that I wished I hadn't hidden in the car until the last possible minute so I wouldn't have to talk to anyone before the event started.

You can access sound bath recordings on any of your favorite places to get music, but I can't recommend a live experience enough. Just leave the chardonnay at home.

BINAURAL BEATS

You may be familiar with optical illusions, but did you know there are also auditory illusions? Binaural beats are one of them. A variation of tones and frequencies, binaural beats are said to help reduce anxiety, increase focus, lower stress, promote relaxation, boost positivity, and assist with pain management. Binaural beats are believed to create brain wave patterns like those experienced in meditation, leading to similar positive effects on your mental and physical health.

There are five known brain frequencies with these associated benefits:

- Delta (1.5–4 Hz) for deep sleep
- Theta (5–8 Hz) for facilitating meditation, increasing creativity, and decreasing anxiety
- Alpha (9–14 Hz) for an additional frequency for decreasing anxiety and increasing relaxation
- Beta (15–40 Hz) for increasing concentration, problem-solving, and memory
- Gamma (30–90 Hz) for enhancing training or learning

Although early studies have shown a correlation between binaural beats and decreased stress, researchers have not determined how well binaural beat therapy works for everyone. Still, the idea of improving your mental health just by putting on headphones is alluring, and binaural beat tracks can be found either free or cheaply anywhere you already get your music.

Binaural beats are also thought to boost creativity and increase focus.

Binaural beats are also thought to boost creativity and increase focus. Feeling more creative and attentive may naturally promote courage. This effect is especially true if you achieve a flow state (see page 196) where everything else tends to fade away as you "get into the zone" of whatever task is at hand.

AUTONOMOUS SENSORY MERIDIAN RESPONSE (ASMR)

Autonomous Sensory Meridian Response (ASMR) is a mysterious phenomenon known to help some people reduce stress and anxiety. In ASMR, certain stimuli—from tapping to whispering to page turning—triggers the sensation of a tingle starting at the back of your head and moving over your shoulders and down your spine.

People who experience ASMR have reported feeling deeply relaxed, with some reporting a floating sensation. Others describe the sensation as a scalp or brain massage.

Some can experience this tingling sensation simply by listening to music or to someone speaking softly in a caring way, as if telling a bedtime story. But not everyone can easily access the benefits of ASMR via sight or sound or identify the trigger stimuli. If you're open to trying ASMR, there are many free online video channels devoted to this, as well as audio-only tracks available on your favorite music platform.

Musical Nostalgia: Create a Courage Playlist

We tend to discover new music in our adolescence, usually via our friends. Bonding over music creates a sense of belonging within certain social groups, and our music choices become intertwined with our identity over time. For me, because the 1990s spanned my entire teens, I am viscerally drawn to grunge, alt-rock, and early electronica—all of which are still very much my jam.

According to something called "reminiscence bump theory," our memory gives greater brain space to who we were and how we lived in our late teens and early twenties. Paired with the fact that new and novel experiences, especially those that are emotionally charged, are more easily committed to memory than boring ones, it's easy to see how music from this time of life could be incredibly powerful.

If you don't already have a playlist or two with songs from your younger days that make you feel like you could conquer the world, create one now! Think about what song was playing when you had your first kiss in the gymnasium at a class dance. Or the song you and your friends played over and over after school. Musical nostalgia is a phenomenon that allows us to reconnect with our adolescent selves in ways that no other activity can replicate.

There is no exact scientific explanation for ASMR, though it has been differentiated from the musical chills sensation called "frisson," as ASMR is relaxing while frisson is arousing.

Early research has shown that ASMR has the potential to reduce stress and anxiety in those who experience it. The calming effects of ASMR can be beneficial for people trying to navigate fear or stressful situations. By allowing you to relax and focus on something soothing, if you can experience ASMR, it can help you re-center yourself and move through to the other side of fear more easily.

Although much of the research on musical nostalgia has been done around the effects of music during adolescence, you can tap into the courage-enhancing energy of a playlist that transports you back to any positive or empowering time in your life. Creating musical nostalgia relieves stress—by recalling positive experiences from your past, you'll be able to draw on those positive emotions, which can help alleviate current feelings of anxiety or depression.

Music can be a more effective and reliable trigger for producing nostalgic feelings than photos, smells, or even food! Upon hearing any song, your auditory cortex is stimulated as your brain processes the information contained within the harmonies, melodies, and rhythms. From there, different parts of your brain join in on the jam, depending on how you choose to interact with the song.

Listening deeply to the lyrics? Then your parietal cortex (responsible for paying attention) will shift into action. Decide you're able to belt out the chorus as well as the lead singer on the track playing in the car? Then your premotor cortex (responsible for planning and then movements) joins in the fun. But most important for our examination here is the amygdala and prefrontal cortex activation you get by listening to a song that triggers an emotionally juicy positive memory, decreasing anxiety and increasing your bold bravery as you tap "start" on your playlist.

A warning: The stimuli presented in these videos and audio tracks are highly idiosyncratic. There will be lots of whispering and playing of some unique "instruments," such as crinkling paper or acrylic nails clicking together. There are even videos of people chewing cookies. Personally, I benefit from ASMR with emotionally evocative music and binaural beats, but many of these more unique offerings make me cringe.

VOCALIZATION

Commonly referred to as the voice box, the larynx houses our vocal cords and is connected to the vagus nerve. When we sing, hum, or chant, we activate the vagus nerve, which sends the "all okay" signal to our nervous system that we're safe and can return to a place of calm. There is no specific decibel level you need to achieve the benefits, and you can get the same vocal stimulation of the vagus nerve by humming, or chanting a sound that reverberates well (like the sound of "om" used in meditation, Hinduism, or Buddhism), or even gargling.

Mind the Gap

Having lived in central London means that I can easily recall the exact sound the automated voice makes on each Underground train you take. "Mind the gap" is meant to warn passengers not to fall into the space between where they are and where they're going. I see *Brave New You*'s neurohacks similarly—they are techniques to help you create enough of a gap between the fear you feel in the moment and your reaction to it, and to give you more control and more space between where you are and where you're going, so you can decide if you should step, jump, or maybe just stay put and wait.

Next time your heart begins to race and you feel the desire to freeze up or run from something you know isn't dangerous, take a leap and try to break free using any one of these biological keys to courage. Fear can give us tunnel vision, making it difficult to think clearly, so I suggest practicing some of your favorites before you step into that uncomfortable space of distress. Action, even a tiny step, leaves us feeling more empowered than staying stuck and stagnant. By definition transformation is change, so if we truly want a different outcome, we need to try different ways of thinking and behaving. The more space you have in between what you feel and what you do allows you to make new, possibly transformational, choices.

Courage is a complex interplay between our biology and our experiences. The anatomical, physiological, and genetic features of our bodies will always influence how we experience life. But the human brain is not unmalleable. We can learn, unlearn, and relearn regardless of our age.

Action, even a tiny step, leaves us feeling more empowered than staying stuck and stagnant.

Plus, who knows where technology will take us!

Already, we're on the cusp of unprecedented breakthroughs in understanding and manipulating our brain, including how we respond to fear. Exciting research advancements are paving the way for us to better harness our courage and conquer the fears that haunt us. Technologies like virtual reality (VR)–assisted fear conditioning, which could potentially revolutionize exposure therapy, and non-invasive brain stimulation techniques like Transcranial Magnetic Stimulation (TMS) are already showing promise in early testing. Who knows, maybe one day we will have the ability to create fully personalized neurohacking strategies tailored to our unique brain structures, life experiences, and fear responses.

But until then, start playing around with these neurohacks to help you "mind the gap."

CHAPTER 10

The Psychological Keys to Courage

Hope and fear cannot occupy the same space. Invite one to stay.
—MAYA ANGELOU

I'm writing this on the twentieth anniversary of NASA's Space Shuttle *Columbia* mission STS-107 breaking apart upon reentry to Earth, resulting in all hands lost.

I, and NASA, would never be the same again.

Working on STS-107 was, and still is, one of the highlights of my life. STS-107 was *Columbia*'s twenty-eighth mission and focused on scientific research as the International Space Station was being built. Commander Rick Husband led the crew to carry out over eighty experiments sent from physical, life, and space sciences teams on Earth. Working around the clock, Michael Anderson, William McCool, David Brown, Laurel Clark, Kalpana Chawla, and Ilan Ramon ensured STS-107's research could boldly go where no experiments had gone before.

On February 1, the crew was set to come home. All was going according to the reentry plan at 8:59 a.m. By 9:00 a.m., Houston had lost all communication with the crew. Twelve minutes later, mission control got a call from a local news station that shuttle debris was falling like stars across the bright blue Texas sky.

Not once while scanning ancient dusty tomes in the NASA Ames bunker library, popping into our hypergravitational lab, or eating lunch at the base of Hangar One—a hangar so large it had its very own weather system—did I ever think that our work would go on the last flight of the Space Shuttle *Columbia*.

After the STS-107 tragedy, I left NASA. Not because there wasn't still more work to do to advance our scientific understanding of life, of course. But after deeply examining the courage of the STS-107 crew I began to really examine my own life and ask, "Am I living the most courageous life possible? Is the level of positive impact I'm making on the world enough for me?" The answer was a resounding "no" to both of those questions, so I left my work at NASA in search of something bolder.

Courage is not the absence of fear, but the willingness and ability to confront it. And wouldn't it be easier and more effective to confront your fears with a set of tools to help?

In the following pages, we'll dive into the psychological keys to courage focused on influencing your thoughts, behaviors, and thinking patterns to improve your daily experiences with fear and courage.

There are many different forms of courage, from physical to psychological, and I would argue that you could find all of them in the STS-107 crew. I would also argue that you could find all the same hues of courage in yourself.

When you're in possession of the right psychological key to unlock your courage, the path to a more fulfilling life becomes much easier to walk.

Connection: Danger Bonding

Connection is a powerful way to build courage and decrease fear in your life, especially when it's with someone who provides a mutually secure attachment (see page 52). I no longer have any blood relations in my life and haven't for years. But I do have a strong circle of friends who became family, and though we don't share a home or even live in the same city, I know I can call on them anytime, anywhere, and they'll be there for me. Just knowing that empowers me to go out in the world and do scary things.

Building relationships as adults can be hard, but one of the quickest ways I've found to forge deep, authentic bonds with people is by asking for help and sharing struggles, especially if there is an element of stress or danger—what I call "danger bonding." When I think about the friends who are my family, I can't help recalling these meet-cute stories that were all steeped in some type of stressful situation.

I met Michelle and Deliah when we were just nineteen, not even old enough to legally drink the cocktails we were serving at the local Elephant Bar, where we bonded over the incredibly stressful environment of the busiest restaurant in town, working eight-hour shifts with zero breaks (it was, uh, the 1990s—labor laws were a bit more lax).

Kristen and I instantly bonded in our thirties after I asked her, a total stranger I had just met in the bathroom, to save me from interacting with a creeper of a guy at a conference we were all attending.

During the very first hour on my very first day out in the world as a newly minted single lady after twelve years with my ex, I met Elaine, who just happened to also be on her very first day out in the world as a newly minted single lady after twelve years with her ex.

Brekke and I became forever friends while she helped shepherd Momma Helen to the other side as her death doula.

Iris and I would bond after an awkward conversation with a career dominatrix at a speakers' conference in Florida.

Michele and I cemented our sistership in the dark bowels of a Los Angeles haunted house during Halloween as we spent our first five minutes of meeting clutching each other and screaming.

In my forties, Stephanie and I met while she was interviewing me for one of my first—and very nervous—guest spots on a science podcast.

Brielan and I found ourselves the only two science pirates in a sea of career marketers.

So many stories of danger bonds that turned into years, sometimes decades of deep, authentic, joyous sistership, all because I had the courage to say hi, reach out a hand, share my own struggles, ask for help, or run away—hand in hand—from a (pretend) ax-wielding murderer together.

To be clear, danger bonding is *not* trauma bonding. Trauma bonding is when someone who is being abused forms a favorable personal connection to their abuser, where they feel sympathy or admiration for the abuser instead of anger or disgust. Stockholm syndrome is an example, when a kidnappee begins to befriend or even defend their kidnapper.

Danger bonding simply decreases the time it takes to go from stranger to friend, spurred on by some level of outward stressor that people can bond over. Other examples of danger bonding would be the lifetime friendships made on a movie set that has an intense and grueling three-month production schedule in the tropical forests of Costa Rica. Or the bond between soldiers or firefighters.

However, if you're looking to expand your circle of friends, you don't have to go off to war or run into a burning building to take advantage of this connection cheat code. Here are a few ideas:

- Take an introductory class in an activity that is a bit more on the extreme side and is totally new to you. Think rock climbing, surfing, or kayaking. Since everyone will be scared of this new activity, you won't be the only one, and a class structure more easily lends itself to chatting up strangers.

- Join a group where you can compete. This doesn't have to be physical—it could also be a hackathon or tabletop gaming. Team structures naturally lend themselves to connection, and competition with other teams adds a bit of that stress spice.

- Join as a solo traveler to an organized small group that aligns with your values and interests. I say solo because when we travel with a partner, we tend to shy away from forming deeper connections with new people. The more new-and-novel the better. Personally, I love G-Adventures for this because the company crafts international trips based on your desired level of activity and general age grouping.

What other ways can you fast-track trust and connection by inserting yourself into situations that require a bit of fear and a bit of courage?

Attachment Practice

Even if you didn't have secure attachments as a child, you can build them as an adult—but it takes time, opportunity, and energy. If a secure attachment relationship with a human isn't currently available to you, don't fret—you can get the same benefits from taking care of animals (Hi Bandit, beloved pooch, I love you!), engaging in spiritual practices, communing with nature, or being in deep service to something greater than yourself.

Here are a few nonhuman-based ways to build courage in connection.

SHINRIN-YOKU

Until relatively recently, humans didn't have to make a conscious effort to include nature in their daily lives, yet many of us now live in big cities with very little green space.

A popular way to mindfully address this concern is through shinrin-yoku, or forest bathing.

Shinrin-yoku began as a concept and practice in Japan in the early 1980s and refers to spending time in nature by taking a leisurely stroll through the forest. Forest bathing is thought to induce a relaxed state, decreasing the body's fight-or-flight response. Regular forest bathing may even have cumulative effects, promoting a calm state even when not walking through nature.

Researchers in a 2019 study found that forest bathing for fifteen minutes decreased participants' heart rates and blood pressure while encouraging a calm state. Another study reported that participants expressed significantly lower anxiety levels after a two-hour forest walk. Lower levels of cortisol and adrenaline were also found in participants after forest bathing.

Forest bathing is thought to induce a relaxed state, decreasing the body's fight-or-flight response.

A significant component of forest bathing is mindfulness, which requires grounding yourself in the present to become more intrinsically and extrinsically aware. Mindfulness is a mental technique studied for its positive effects on fear extinction, or the reduction of a conditioned fear response. So it's plausible that with forest bathing, where fear-reducing mindfulness is combined with the relaxing act of being in nature, you could decrease your fears over a particular act or thing and arrive at a calmer state.

There are even preliminary studies looking into the value of virtual reality shinrin-yoku. Though there is nothing quite like being in nature, the wild is not accessible to everyone, depending on physical abilities, geographic location, access to transportation, or having the means to pay for travel. So, VR forest bathing may be a future option for big-city school, medical, or library programs.

JARDINER

From the French word for "gardening," jardiner is a way to decrease your everyday fear arousal by getting your hands dirty in a garden. One study found that when participants were asked to perform outdoor gardening for thirty minutes, their stress levels significantly decreased, while their positive mood increased. Keep in mind that they were not performing excessively demanding tasks like moving heavy branches. Instead, they engaged in light pruning, weeding, sowing, and planting during the Northern Hemisphere spring when the weather was cloudy and dry. The participants' self-reported stress levels and measured salivary cortisol levels improved after gardening.

Researchers believe there are a few reasons for these results. First, moderate exercise has been shown to reduce stress levels. For most, gardening is a form of light to moderate exercise that increases physical activity without being too strenuous. Research also shows that contact with nature has the capacity to reduce stress levels (see the "Shinrin-yoku" section on page 188).

And because gardening is an outdoor task, it exposes gardeners to the sights and sounds of nature while providing some much-needed sunlight-induced vitamin D production. It's important to note also that gardening is a goal-directed task, which can increase feelings of positivity and empowerment. Experts theorize that goal-directed tasks increase the likelihood that individuals will regularly interact with nature, receiving its stress-relieving benefits not once, but continually.

GRATITUDE

Having a gratitude practice can help you become more optimistic, reduce stress, boost your immune system, and decrease feelings of loneliness. Cultivating gratitude means affirming the good things that have come your way and acknowledging how others can infuse your life with goodness. The art of gratitude and its benefits go hand in hand. But practicing gratitude has also been associated with decreased fear and increased courage.

The benefits of gratitude

Scientists believe that when we recognize something good in our lives our brains secrete higher amounts of dopamine, the neurotransmitter associated with pleasure and reward, which leads to an increase in overall happiness. Dopamine is most associated with your brain's "reward center," though it has other roles, too. It has been linked with modulating emotional resilience—that is, how well your body can manage stress, fear, and crisis and then return to pre-crisis mode. It's also a necessary foundation for developing things like self-esteem and bravery. Gratitude in the face of opposition, even the most minor setbacks, may boost your ability to bounce back and approach future situations more confidently.

Studies show that those who regularly practice gratitude are more resilient to physical health issues (such as heart failure, inflammation, and depression) and have lower levels of perceived stress. In fact, a study of firefighters showed that those with a more grateful disposition and who actively practiced gratitude were found to be less stressed and experienced less burnout than those who did not, leading to better mental and physical health outcomes.

Creating a gratitude practice

No matter how you personally define gratitude, most people will agree that a gratitude practice is rooted in regularly reflecting on, and expressing feelings of, thankfulness about your life experiences, your privileges, and the people who are important to you. Though it's not always easy to find moments of gratitude in the midst of your toughest challenges, doing so can bolster you in being open to future experiences and opportunities. Although it can be a series of starts and stops at first, research suggests that by engaging in activities like journaling and meditation, which help you connect with your feelings of gratitude, you create new neural pathways that make you more likely to experience these positive emotions in the future.

To get started, first get clear on what brings you joy. Start by writing down all the things that bring you pleasure—simple things like sunshine, nature walks, petting puppies, or spending time with friends and loved ones, or bigger things like career successes or travel experiences. This will help remind you of all there is to be grateful for in your life as you begin your practice.

Here are some things I do to sneak in mini moments of gratitude throughout my day that you can experiment with for yourself:

• **Gratitude shares:** I like to snap pictures of things that I see throughout the day that bring me joy or that I'm grateful for and text these pics to my friends. This helps me keep my social bonds strong, and I think of it as a way of spreading gratitude and positivity to those I care about in an authentic way that feeds our bond in our ever-chaotic lives. The last three gratitude shares in my phone are a photo of my rescue dog, Bandit; with his yellow duckie toy in his mouth, the first bee I saw in the New Year, and a photo of my favorite flavor of bubble water—coconut—in stock at the store.

• **"You win or you learn":** I've seen this quote attributed to a few different sources. It's about learning to view challenges from a different perspective. Consider a difficulty you faced recently and try writing down an important lesson that emerged from it. This exercise helps you reframe challenges as opportunities instead of obstacles. When faced with a challenge in life, such as an illness or a financial difficulty, it can be easy to get caught up in negative thoughts about what could or should have been. This one isn't always easy, but with practice it can help you cultivate gratitude and appreciation even in difficult situations.

- **Hooray for today:** Celebrate the small wins, too. Whether it's making progress on an important project or simply surviving a tough day, take time to celebrate all of your accomplishments!

Gratitude is a powerful practice for bringing more joy into our lives—and there are so many ways to weave it into your routine. The suggestions above are just a start. If none of these resonate with you, the UC Berkeley Greater Good Science Center is a great next stop for even more ideas.

FILL YOUR COURAGE JAR

A courage jar can be a powerful way to boost your confidence and bravery during difficult times by drawing on your past successes. Your courage jar can be a Mason jar, a box, or any other container. Mine is an ornate Victorian monstrosity that makes me feel like I'm a dowager countess living in a castle full of books and ghosts. The idea is that whenever you do something courageous, you're going to jot down a note about it and add it to your courage jar.

Then, when you need a boost or on some predetermined date, you will take all the scraps of paper out of your jar and read about all the ways you've lived bravely. I like to combine my courage jar with the power of rituals by reading the notes in my jar at the end of the year and then starting a new jar on January 1.

It can be easy to discount and dismiss all the ways that we are brave each day. But keeping a courage jar serves as a constant visual reminder of how far you've come on your journey to living more boldly. Regularly contributing to your jar can strengthen your self-esteem, decrease stress, and help with managing anxiety and depression by providing positive reinforcement when you need it.

Gratitude is a powerful practice for bringing more joy into our lives—and there are so many ways to weave it into your routine.

The physical act of writing down something positive also helps solidify and affirm it in your mind, which can increase your resilience in the face of hardship. Having tangible, everyday reminders of our courage is key—taking just one minute to write down something positive will help solidify these feelings and make them more lasting over time.

The Power of Play

When was the last time you played?

No, silly, I'm not talking about scrolling through social media or binge-watching your newest favorite show. I'm talking about real, unadulterated playtime.

Take a moment to pause and think back to happy childhood moments of spending the entire day playing. When I do this, I think about the freedom I felt jumping on my small trampoline. Or playing with my Barbie pool, which was only allowed as a special treat because of the mess I would make splashing about in our living room (please don't ask me why Momma Helen didn't just shoo me out to the porch). Or how I would swing in dappled sunshine until the day grew dark.

The more life's demands increase, the less time we spend playing when, in fact, making time for play would actually help us deal better with the trepidation and agony of life's daily challenges.

The more life's demands increase, the less time we spend playing when, in fact, making time for play would actually help us deal better with the trepidation and agony of life's daily challenges.

Working hard and being productive takes its toll on us, and unfettered play can be a soothing balm because it increases activation of the anterior cingulate cortex (ACC), which improves our ability to regulate our emotions. Uniquely positioned in the brain, the ACC has connections to both the logic-driven prefrontal cortex and the emotion-driven limbic system. The ACC serves a critical role in how our life experiences are committed to memory as fears.

In short, activating your ACC can improve your ability to regulate your emotions and better process your own personal fears.

The type of play should be enjoyable to you, eliciting overall net positive emotions. Of course, you can be frustrated some of the time, especially during skill building, but overall you should leave the game feeling pleasure and renewal. As an added bonus, if you can step into a flow state where you are enjoying the activity so much you lose track of time, that's even better because where flow goes, fear cannot follow.

PLAY AS A BALM FOR DEPRESSION AND ANXIETY

Play provides us with fun and relaxation and has many psychological benefits that can help us become more courageous in our daily lives. Research shows that adults who regularly engaged in playful activities experienced lower levels of depression and anxiety than those who did not engage in play. Whether your form of play involves making art or playing music, games, or sports, actively engaging in playful activities can help reduce stress levels and improve psychological well-being. It's important to note that you only reap the benefits when you are the one playing the game, as opposed to watching others play.

When we play, we also activate the Default Mode Network, which is associated with more expansive thought, empathy, imagination, and creativity. Through fMRI studies, researchers were able to observe two distinct sets of interacting brain regions: the Default Mode Network and the Task Positive Network. For ease, I will simply refer to them as Default Mode or Task Positive. These two networks function in opposition of each other, meaning when one is active, the other is not. When we're focused on our to-do list (tasks), attempting to use logic to solve problems, or concerned with perceived threats, our Task Positive is at the helm. When this happens,

Finding Your Flow State

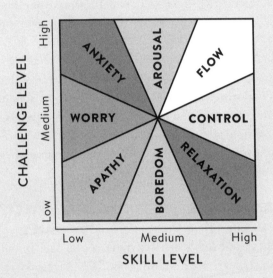

Have you ever lost track of time doing something that wasn't easy, but you felt confident you could do it? If so, you were in flow state!

Popularized by the work of Mihaly Csikszentmihalyi and Jeanne Nakamura, "flow" is defined as a state of dynamic equilibrium where your skills and abilities are in harmony with the level of difficulty or challenge you're facing. When you enter flow, your abilities consistently meet the tasks set before you, but you feel neither bored nor overwhelmed.

From playing music to sports, from hiking to video games, we can get into a flow state with any activity that brings us joy and offers the right balance of challenge. On top of the enjoyment of a flow state, research has shown that it also decreases overall stress anxiety since your brain can't simultaneously be in a state of fear *and* in a state of flow.

Where flow goes, courage follows.

the Task Positive tends to activate your sympathetic nervous system, resulting in you feeling stressed.

In short, Default Mode activation equals big, expansive thoughts and imaginings with less stressful feelings. Task Positive activation means the "get er done" mode of becoming stressed and hyper-focused on threats and tasks.

By activating the Default Mode (thus deactivating the Task Positive), play helps reduce fear by providing a distraction from negative thinking patterns and shifting our focus away from perceived threats. Fearful thoughts often cause us to become bogged down in worry and anxiety. By engaging in net-positive playful activities such as games or art without ambition, our attention is diverted away from these negative thoughts and toward something far more enjoyable and uplifting. This allows us to enjoy the moment instead of worrying about the future.

By engaging in net-positive playful activities such as games or art without ambition, our attention is diverted away from these negative thoughts and toward something far more enjoyable and uplifting.

PLAYING NICE WITH OTHERS

When we play, our brains release dopamine and serotonin, making us feel more relaxed and happier, which can reduce our stress levels. As an added bonus, when we engage with others while playing games, our brains release oxytocin—the trust and connection hormone—helping us build stronger relationships with those around us, which further bolsters the stress-reducing powers of play. When we play we can decrease our fear arousal, making it easier to tap into our creativity and our ability to come up with innovative solutions to our biggest problems. Through play we learn how to take risks without feeling overwhelmed or intimidated, which can translate to more capacity for risk-taking behavior in other areas of life.

Play also encourages social interaction, which can help reduce feelings of isolation and loneliness associated with fear. The act of sharing experiences with others through play creates a sense of community, which helps diminish feelings of insecurity and vulnerability typically associated with fearful situations. When we feel understood by those around us, it helps us feel more secure and less scared overall.

"You Are What You Think"

A version of this quote has been attributed to a wide variety of sources, from Buddha to the Athenian Stoics of the third century BCE to Ralph Waldo Emerson. Regardless of where the credit lies, the truth of this quote influences every aspect of our cognition, especially our emotions.

Early thinking on the subject completely separated emotions and cognition into two separate systems. Now we better understand that the two are far more dynamic, with our emotions having a substantial influence on our perception, attention, learning, memory, reasoning, and problem-solving (collectively referred to as cognition). You can think of cognition as a system focused on being proactive and forward looking, while our emotions live in the land of reactivity.

We can use thoughts to encourage ourselves, build confidence, reduce fear and anxiety, and ultimately live with more courage and less fear.

How we perceive the world and the way we talk to ourselves has a tangible impact on just about all facets of our lives. And taming our inner monologues can be incredibly difficult. We very much create our own realities through the power of thought, then use those thoughts to shape who we are and will become. We can use thoughts to encourage ourselves, build confidence, reduce fear and anxiety,

Bravery Break: Spiraling Thought Journal

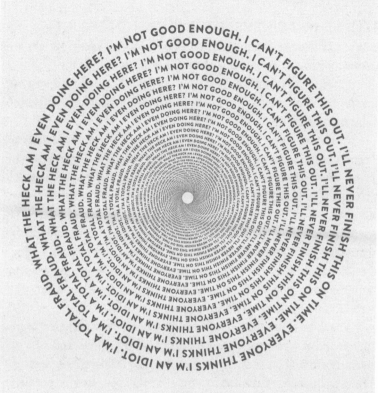

Unsurprisingly, we tend to gravitate toward the same negative thought patterns when our fear is aroused. Try to catch yourself when you start the negative self-talk and write down what you're saying to yourself in the shape of an actual spiral. Sure, you could type it into your notes function, but the act of physically writing it down in a way that you wouldn't normally write (in the shape of a spiral) helps provide the jolt you need to snap you out of the pattern. It can be any shape, really, but the spiral shape also reminds you that you are not your negative thoughts and not to believe everything you think.

and ultimately live with more courage and less fear. Thoughts can have a powerful influence on how we live our lives, either as paralyzing forces or as supportive mechanisms for transformation.

BELIEVE TO ACHIEVE: THE PYGMALION EFFECT

One of my favorite childhood rhymes is one we all know: "Sticks and stones may break my bones, but words will never hurt me."

I'm sorry to report that this is a total lie! The way we speak and act toward each other and ourselves absolutely impacts our ability to be successful.

First coined by Robert Rosenthal and Lenore Jacobson, the Pygmalion effect is a psychological phenomenon that reveals the power of our beliefs. In their double-blind study, researchers told participating teachers that certain students were "intellectual late bloomers," and despite their early poor performance, the researchers predicted they would outperform the current top students. Of course this was a total lie, but the teachers in the study didn't know that. The truth was that the students chosen as late-blooming future geniuses were picked completely at random to test the power of the perceptions of others on performance.

Teachers returned to finish out the school year with the "secret" knowledge of who was a late-blooming future genius and who was just a normie. Teachers began treating the "chosen" students differently. Instead of treating them like the poor performers they believed them to be before the intervention, the teachers treated them like they were superstars that just needed a little more encouragement and support. The once-struggling "chosen ones" ended up outperforming their peers, proving that expectations can indeed shape outcomes.

How we are treated and how we perceive ourselves has documented, empirical power.

In essence, the study was the first of many to suggest that what we believe or expect of others can influence their behavior, leading them to behave in ways that confirm our beliefs. It's a self-fulfilling prophecy of sorts, one that plays out in classrooms, workplaces, and all types of relationships.

Though the concept was born out of an education setting, it's applicable across all swaths of life. Take, for example, a trusting, supportive manager who believes there are no weak links on her team versus a micromanaging nightmare of a leader who assumes everyone is incompetent but themselves. The former is likely to foster a more creative, high-performing team because she treats them as valuable, skilled, and capable. The latter will most likely have a team rife with distrust and resentment, leading to a lack of motivation for members to fully apply their talents and skills.

If you can transform your expectations from fear based to courage based, your behavior toward yourself and others reflects those expectations, leading to braver choices and a more courageous mind.

Which team do you think will have better overall outcomes?

Your beliefs and expectations of yourself and others clearly play an important role in your future success. We naturally strive to meet expectations for a simple reason: We desire approval and recognition from others. We might also act differently around others we see as more capable than we are, which could also lead to motivation and improvement within ourselves. Plus, if we think someone can do great things, we often provide more resources and opportunities than before—which could further help someone reach their potential.

Your perception of reality is incredibly powerful. What expectations, from yourself and from trusted others, do you find limiting? How can you rewrite those limiting expectations into something more empowering? If you can transform your expectations from fear based to courage based, your behavior toward yourself and others reflects those expectations, leading to braver choices and a more courageous mind.

Words certainly have the power to hurt, but they also have great power to heal.

RESTRUCTURE AND REFRAME

The first time I spoke about reframing was in front of the TEDx audience in London for my "Myth of Fearlessness" talk. I had reworked my speech, my slides, and even my outfit what felt like countless times. As the speaker before me took the stage, I waited in the darkened wings while my lavalier mic was pinned to my dress. With just a minute or two before I would walk on stage, my mic died. The entire setup had to be changed quickly, and the production assistant, flustered by the tech failure, unhooked the back of my dress along with my non-functioning mic. I was waiting in an open wing at the time, so the audience could see me off to the side if they looked.

With a squeak, I grabbed the back of my dress as the production assistant stage whispered apologies and tried to be "helpful" by fixing my dress with one hand while holding the mic with the other. With twenty seconds left on the clock until I needed to walk on stage, I fumbled to get my dress back in place as he strapped a fresh mic on me. With no time to test and no time to re-center myself I was called on stage, where I felt I might just pass out in front of the packed theater.

As I willed the tiny shoes I had forced my feet into that morning to move forward when the only thing my amygdala wanted to do was run backward, my internal monologue went a little like this: "I can't believe that just happened. It's an omen. I remember nothing. I'm stupid and ugly and should just walk off stage. Is my dress even closed in the back? Am I about to flash the entire TED crowd? Everyone is going to hate me. Okay fine, I'll actually just pass out."

Luckily, dear reader, I did not pass out.

Resigned to my fate, I put my right toe on the X that marked the spot I should stand, looked out into the dark crowd, and finally remembered that I knew what to do. I had tools.

During the few seconds of applause, I did a quick reframe by transforming the litany of negative self-talk into one simple mantra:

"Give that powerful energy to the crowd. Give that powerful energy to the crowd."

Not only did saying this stop my spiraling fear arousal, but it also shifted my focus from my experience to my role in service to the people who had shown up that day to share their time and energy with me. I moved the physical sensations away from the fear I was feeling stuck in myself to the positive energy I wanted to share; recalibrating what had just happened from a potentially disastrous snafu to an opportunity to serve others allowed me to start right on cue (and yes, it turned out, my backside was fully covered, both literally and figuratively).

Reframing is not about making every negative thought a positive one; it's about placing an unhelpful thought into the light of reality.

Reframing is a cognitive technique that actively changes one's perspective on an experience or situation. It encourages you to view an event from a different angle and shift your focus away from problems and toward solutions. Reframing is not about making every negative thought a positive one; it's about bringing an unhelpful thought into the light of reality. Instead of finding the bright side, find meaning. Toxic positivity, a "don't-worry-be-happy-all-the-time-no-matter-what" mentality, is exhausting and incredibly unhelpful in the long term because it makes a habit of ignoring or invalidating your emotions. Reframing is about recognizing the fearful events in your life and responding differently.

Cognitive restructuring and reframing are very similar. Both concepts involve shifting mindsets to view situations from different perspectives. The terms are often used interchangeably, as both are employed to modify faulty or distorted beliefs. The difference lies in how each concept is viewed. Reframing is often seen as something that can be done on your own as you redefine your experience. In contrast, restructuring is often viewed as a therapeutic process involving steps and practice, performed by a professional in a therapy setting.

The first step in reframing is to identify automatic thoughts by observing and documenting moments and situations that trigger a fearful reaction. What thoughts arose in response to that situation? What were the emotions that followed those thoughts? How did you behave?

Once your fears or irrational beliefs have been identified, you can challenge those false ideas and replace them with more realistic or supportive ones as you reframe how you talk to yourself. A few options include:

1. **Self-affirmations:** Talk yourself through difficult situations (I enjoy repeating "I am safe").

2. **Eating the elephant one bite at a time:** Break down whatever overwhelms you into smaller, manageable chunks that don't seem so scary.

3. **Turn your amygdala into a character:** Another way to reframe is to anthropomorphize (or animate) your amygdala into a character. As I've mentioned, I'm a big Marvel fan, so thinking of my amygdala as the overprotective, sometimes bumbling Thor helps me reframe my experience. When I separate the anatomical center of my fear-arousal response from the definition of "me" and turn it into a character, it's easy for me to have conversations with it. For example, I might say, "Okay, Thor, it's cool—you can stop being all aggressive right now, everyone is safe," or "Alrighty Thor, no need to make it all sweaty in here, everyone is safe."

   I know this may sound silly—but that's the point. There is power in letting playfulness replace fear.

THE FAIRY TALE REWRITE
When you think of a fairy tale, what comes to mind?

Before Disney made Cinderella or Snow White into animated classics, these stories plus hundreds more were collected by folklorists Wilhelm Carl Grimm and Jacob Ludwig Carl Grimm, known collectively as the Brothers Grimm. Between 1812 and 1815, the Brothers Grimm set out to collect and study the stories that captured the imagination and beliefs of the German people. From these mostly oral stories, they would publish their best-known work, *Kinder- und Hausmärchen*, or *Grimm's Fairy Tales*. In addition to being entertaining escapism, *Grimm's Fairy Tales* have been used to teach values such as courage and perseverance to young readers for generations, helping them understand difficult concepts in an easily digestible way by sparking their imaginations.

In the exercise below, you will tap into the power of what I call "the fairy tale rewrite" to bolster your bravery. The idea here is to take a fear-based origin story from your past, examine it, and then rewrite this story with a new courageous ending from an objective third-person perspective. This benevolent writer wants the best for all characters involved, especially you, the hero.

I'll walk you through this step-by-step using my own fairy tale rewrite as a model for how your story might unfold. Creating this alternative narrative, even if you feel it's silly or not a believable story, will boost your courage by strengthening your anterior cingulate cortex (ACC).

Step 1: Write your shitty first draft

In *Bird by Bird*, author Anne Lamott introduces readers to the idea of the "shitty first draft" as a way to move through perfectionism and improve your writing. In this first step, you're going to write a shitty first draft of your fear-based origin story—the story of a pivotal moment in your life that didn't go as well as it could have (or maybe it was downright tragic), and that has come to limit your self-belief in some way.

My fear story dates way back to the third grade, though I still recall what happened in crisp detail. I was one of those unlucky kids who had all sorts of dental issues, including a palate that was too small to accommodate all my adult teeth. However, I was fortunate enough to have good dental insurance, which meant I had a palate expander installed on the roof of my mouth. It was a medieval torture device that Momma Helen had to stick a tiny key into each night to expand its width ever so slightly while I slept. When I first had it installed, I struggled to speak clearly until I got accustomed to having this foreign thing in my mouth. So when I spoke, it sounded a bit like someone was holding my tongue between their fingers.

In my third-grade classroom, one of the big privileges was to be the student who got to answer the class phone when the front office called. As a chatty child, I loved doing this. That is, until my teacher publicly ostracized me for the way I sounded the day after having my palate expander inserted.

After answering the phone and perfectly repeating the official classroom script, my teacher yelled across the student-filled room, "Mary, don't answer the phone. You talk funny."

Of course I wanted to be anywhere but there at that moment, clenching a phone receiver in my tiny hands, with thirty pairs of eyes passing judgment after being othered by the most respected person in the room. Moments like these color how we perceive ourselves and the world. They can stay with us for decades—until we rewrite them.

For this exercise, identify a fear story from your life that you want to rewrite, something similar to my "You Talk Funny" tale. This can be a story that has lived rent-free in your mind for years or a new one that has been dominating your thoughts. It can be a short statement you find true about yourself or the world, or it can be longer. Jot down whatever comes to mind about where your fear story came from. Begin by writing a "shitty first draft" that recounts what happened to you. Write your story in third person, so that you become a character.

For example:

One day, a young girl named Mary had to have a dental device placed on the roof of her mouth because there wasn't enough room for all her adult teeth to come in. She loved to laugh and talk and sing. When she first got the device it felt strange, and when she spoke she

Choose one memorable event you wish had gone better, where you could have shown up with more courage. Then answer these prompts:

- What is one of your strengths that shines through when you think back on that memory?

- Since you chose this as your first experience, it serves as a valuable learning opportunity. List what lessons you can draw from it.

- Is there a particular aspect of the experience that you could possibly feel proud of? What did you do right?

- Lastly, envision an alternate reality. How would you alter your thoughts, reactions, or behaviors if you could go back in time? Let your imagination roam free and consider how this experience could be shaped differently if you had the power to rewrite it.

sounded a bit different to her own ears. But she paid no attention and spent the rest of the day playing outside.

When she went to school the next day, something very exciting happened. The class phone rang and she was the closest to it—which meant she got to answer it. Following all the rules the teacher had taught her class, she picked up the phone and said, "Hello, this is Miss Jenny's room. How may I help you?" Suddenly, from across the room, in a loud, booming voice, Miss Jenny bellowed out, "Mary, don't answer the phone—you talk funny."

The little girl stood frozen, the beige phone with its curling cord in hand, as the entire class turned to look. Miss Jenny snatched the phone from Mary and pointed for her to return to her seat. Under the stares and snickers of her classmates, with her head held low, *she returned to her seat . . . silenced and sad. In the end, the little girl learned that to use her voice was to receive the wrath of those in charge and the ire of her peers. That day she vowed never to speak up in class, or anywhere else, ever again.*

Step 2: Outline the details of your new story

Now that you have your shitty first draft written, you're going to sketch an outline of your new story. The goal is to keep it simple and straightforward, like something you'd write for a young reader. So skip the flowery language and boil your tale down to the following basic parts:

Your main characters: Identify your main characters, both good and bad. As the protagonist (the good guy), you should be the brave and resourceful hero, while the antagonist (villain) in your story should be formidable but able to be defeated. These "good" and "bad" characters should exhibit traits that match their roles. For example, the antagonist may display selfishness or greed, while the antagonist could be kind or generous. Real humans are complex, but for the purposes of this exercise we want our storybook versions to be simple.

In my story, the characters I identified were Princess Mary (me) and the Evil Queen Jenny (my teacher, Miss Jenny).

Your magical setting: Fairy tales need an element of magic or fantasy. This could take the form of magical creatures, such as fairies or talking animals or fantastical worlds like enchanted forests or underwater kingdoms. Along the way, the hero may encounter magical creatures or helpful allies who will aid them on their journey. Adding this level of whimsy helps de-escalate the fear or shame you've attached to this deeply personal story of yours.

My magical setting: I'm envisioning a Harry Potter-at-Hogwarts-style-castle classroom.

Your goals and obstacles: In your story, there should also be obstacles that you must overcome before reaching the end, such as dragons or evil witches intent on thwarting your efforts. Also, what is the one clear goal your protagonist strives for to reach a happy ending? You can make this a literal goal or a metaphorical one.

My goal: to share my voice with others. My obstacle: Evil Queen Jenny's damaging words.

Your transformation: Fairy tales are inherently about transformation. A strong story arc should take the protagonist from one state to another, often leaving home in search of adventure and returning triumphant.

My transformation: I want to rewrite the transformation from *I'm afraid of sounding inadequate/not good enough when I speak* to "I will speak my mind even if my voice shakes" (a quote by author and activist Maggie Kuhn).

Your new happy ending: Finally, your story should come full circle with a resolution—and a positive one to help rewire the event toward a positive outcome. Happy endings are a must for your fairy tale rewrite. After all, fairy tales typically end with the villain vanquished and the protagonist in a happier place than when they started. Write the happiest, bravest new ending to your story you can imagine

My new happy ending: Instead of feeling embarrassed and slinking off in shame to my seat, never to speak up in that class again, my new happy ending is for Princess Mary to stand up to the Evil Queen in the moment and say, with strength and pride, "This is how I talk. This is who I am. I am worthy of speaking to others."

Step 3: Time to rewrite!

This step is about pulling yourself out of that old fear-based story and rewriting it in classic fairy-tale structure. Begin with "Once upon a time" and move to "and then this happened . . . and then this happened . . . and in the end _____." Similar to your shitty first draft, your fairy-tale rewrite should be written in third person with "you" as a character. The idea behind rewriting your fear story as a fairy tale is that this form allows you to more easily feel compassion for the main character (you), and to pick out the injustice while imagining what the next chapter will look like when the heroine (you) is victorious.

My new story, with my fairy-tale rewrite, looks like this:

Once upon a time, a little princess named Mary had to have an evil-looking dental device placed on the roof of her mouth because she was so tiny that there wasn't enough room for all her adult teeth. She loved to laugh and talk and sing. When she got the device it felt strange at first, and when she spoke, she sounded a bit different to her own ears, but she paid no attention and spent the rest of the day playing in the garden.

When she went to school the next day, something very exciting happened. The phone in her magical castle classroom rang, and, since she was the closest to the phone, she got to answer it. Following all the rules the teacher had taught her class, she picked up the phone and began to speak. Suddenly, from across the room in a loud, booming voice, the Evil Queen Jenny bellowed, "Mary, don't answer the phone! You talk funny."

Knowing her worth and the power of her voice, no matter how funny it sounded, Princess Mary stood tall and said, "This is how I talk. This is who I am. I am worthy of speaking to others. We are all worthy in this classroom" The Evil Queen was so surprised that she said nothing as her jaw went slack from shock. The other students erupted in cheers and chants of "We are worthy! We are worthy!" as the Evil Queen left the classroom without another word.

Okay, your turn! Rewrite your fear story with a simple hero, a villain, something wanted, and at least one instance where the hero is attacked, tested, helped, or challenged in some way. Your rewrite can be short or long—it's your story, tell it how you want! Just make sure to write it in the third person, and don't forget a happy ending.

You're Not Flawed; You're Not Broken

When professional psychotherapy moved away from being dominated by the Freudian "painful emotions are all caused by your childhood experiences" model to the cognitive behavioral therapy (CBT) model of "our thoughts impact our feelings," there was a revolution in how we viewed the human emotional experience.

So much of early psychology was based on the faulty premise that the human mind is weak and broken. But that couldn't be further from the truth. Yes, of course, there are pathologies and disorders of the mind that need more support than any book could provide. But there is power in shifting our mindset from "fixing a broken machine" to "learning how to optimize your unique and powerful brain." One of the ways you can optimize the functioning of your brain is through your thoughts.

> By empowering yourself to shift your thinking patterns, you can change the way you perceive fear and courage.

When you change your thoughts, you change your emotions.

We will always have emotional reactions to the ups and downs and twists and turns of life. But how we react to them and the tools we use to navigate them is within our control. By empowering yourself to shift your thinking patterns, you can change the way you perceive fear and courage. You can instill in yourself a sense of self-efficacy, helping yourself see actionable steps forward so you can more firmly believe in your ability to weather any fear storm you encounter.

You are in control of your story. Now that you've been armed with awareness and knowledge, who will you become?

CHAPTER 11

A More Courageous Tomorrow

I believe I am powerful, therefore I am.
—*KINGDOM OF THE FEARED*
BY KERRI MANISCALCO

What kind of world happens when we learn to live as bolder, braver, and more courageous versions of ourselves? Imagine a reality where we're all taking the risks needed to make our dreams come true. A world where people are inspired by each another's stories, where they support one another, and cheer on their successes. A world where nobody is afraid to speak up, stand out, or try something new.

When we step into our courage, our whole world becomes stronger and more resilient. We can combat fear-based narratives and work toward solving big global issues such as environmental sustainability, poverty, gender equality, racism, and more. Taking risks also helps us become more creative and innovative, which we'll need to be in order to solve our biggest problems. We can develop new products, services, and technologies that make people's lives better. Whether it's finding a cure for diseases or developing renewable energy sources to solve climate change, every new idea has the potential to benefit society as a whole.

Individually, living bravely means being willing to confront uncomfortable situations and have difficult conversations. It's about speaking up when we know something is wrong, and working together to find solutions. When you have the courage to face your own fears head-on, you contribute to creating an environment of understanding, respect, and empathy all around you—qualities that are essential for creating a peaceful world where everyone is treated with dignity and respect.

Now imagine a world where everyone was comfortable navigating their greatest fears instead of denying and repressing them, then taking them out on themselves or others. We could make tough decisions without the fear of failure driving our choices. Resources would be allocated with intentionality and creativity instead of from worry or dread. Schools would prioritize curriculums that focus on critical thinking rather than rote memorization, and workplaces would be less toxic and more productive. In short, our communities would be stronger, healthier, and more vibrant for everyone.

Throughout your life, you've faced many challenges that tested your bravery and resilience. Regardless of how you think you did in those moments, be proud that you've been through some difficult times, yet here you are still living courageously—even if it doesn't feel like it.

By reading this book, you now have a deeper understanding of the fear/courage paradox and the wisdom to turn every moment of bravery into lasting change. You now have the tools you need to lean into discomfort and take risks, even if they feel daunting at first—confident in the knowledge that you trust yourself enough to make courageous choices. That doing so will bring far greater rewards than staying in your comfort zone.

When we live with more courage, we reach our goals, learn new things, and navigate our lives toward our personal north star that means the most. We have healthier relationships with ourselves and with others. Worry about the past or the future no longer rules our day or dictates our decisions.

The journey toward living with courage is not an easy road, but it is a path worth taking.

The Pillars of Courageous Living

Remember, courage isn't something you either have or don't have—it's an ongoing process that requires practice, commitment, resilience, and self-compassion. This is where the "pillars of courageous living" come in: They are principles to strive for, not something to perfect but rather embrace. They are four simple ideas to keep front of mind when thinking about taking risks and being willing to make mistakes—and to appreciate the instructive stumbles that result.

PILLAR #1: EMBRACING VULNERABILITY

Vulnerability is the willingness to be open with yourself and those you trust. It happens when you're honest about your feelings and emotions without fear of judgment or criticism. When you embrace your vulnerabilities—your fears, your insecurities, your worries—you're allowing yourself to be seen and heard. You're giving the people around you permission to understand and relate to you on a deeper level.

Vulnerability is necessary for growth because it challenges us to become stronger and wiser. We can choose to boldly face challenges with bravery instead of fear by accepting difficult emotions like disappointment and embarrassment without trying to mask or ignore them. Being vulnerable feels risky because it is! It can be difficult to let down your many guards and share your true self with others, or to be fully honest with yourself. But to live truly courageously, the masks must come off when we show up for ourselves and for others.

PILLAR #2: FINDING STRENGTH IN UNCERTAINTY

Life is uncertain—that will not change. We can't know what the future holds, but we can learn to embrace uncertainty and to find strength within it. Because we prefer certainty and structure over ambiguity, uncertain situations can make us want to retreat or shut down. Our minds tend to go into overdrive when we're uncertain, conjuring up worst-case scenarios and imagining possible outcomes that are often out of proportion to reality.

But when faced with uncertainty, rather than reacting as you've always done, you can take a step back and just observe. This can help you remain grounded in the present moment in lieu of living in hypothetical futures. It's normal to feel unsure. However, being empowered to focus on what you *can* control and turn your attention away from things that you can't allows you to build greater strength and resilience.

PILLAR #3: CULTIVATING SELF-COMPASSION

Try to always extend kindness and understanding to yourself when you make mistakes or encounter difficulties. When you recognize your own pain and respond compassionately rather than punishing yourself for perceived failures or shortcomings, you can use your energy for better things besides suffering. Research reveals that developing self-compassion helps us take better care of ourselves, cope better with difficult emotions, have greater emotional resilience, and ultimately make decisions from a place of strength, not fear.

> *Try to always extend kindness and understanding to yourself when you make mistakes or encounter difficulties.*

When you practice self-compassion, you give yourself permission to accept your weaknesses and failures without judgment. In this way, you recognize your flaws without rendering them unforgivable or insurmountable. Self-compassion allows us to pick ourselves up after failure instead of wallowing in guilt or shame indefinitely.

PILLAR #4: CREATING MEANINGFUL CONNECTIONS

We are wired for connection, but we aren't always able to form meaningful relationships with others. The human brain is unique in its ability to learn about the threats in our environment via social interactions, such as the stories we consume. This adaptive ability means we don't need to experience the actual scary situation to have a lifetime of fear about it (hello *Jaws*, which made a generation afraid to swim in the ocean). Left unchecked and unexamined, it's easy to go down an unhealthy path of developing robust fears based on imagined things—or getting conditioned by the stories you hear—without ever actually experiencing them.

Though that is the darker side of connection, being in community also has the ability to bolster courage and heal from suffering.

Courage in Connection

"I can do it myself!"

This defiant cry, so common among toddlers and preschoolers, is something some of us hold onto for a lifetime when we lean into habits of hyper-independence.

Many psychologists and theorists believe hyper-independence is harmful for both individuals and society as a whole. Many of us keep looking for comfort and connection while being anxious—even terrified—about exploring how it would feel to share our emotional reality with another person and develop a deep relationship through that connection. So, we avoid such connections. Why? Despite wanting and needing them, we greatly fear rejection, which often tempts us to avoid connection. But in experiencing two-way empathetic connection, we learn how to express understanding for others and accept understanding in return. This allows us to reclaim the interdependence that makes us human as we unlearn the cultural assumption that we must disconnect to protect ourselves.

Just as we can learn to fear from our daily social interactions with others, we can also become more courageous. According to research, one of the most powerful tools we have when it comes to mastering fear is also the one becoming increasingly more difficult for technocentric humans: experiencing a true, deep connection with another person. When you connect with others, among many other wonderful things that can happen, your fear-arousal system relaxes as it perceives safety in numbers.

Even before the pandemic, adults young and old were experiencing what US Surgeon General Dr. Vivek Murthy called an "epidemic of loneliness." A 2009 study reported that one in five adults felt intense and long-lasting loneliness, and in a 2021 national survey, Harvard found that this number was now two in five, with even higher rates in young adults (61 percent) and mothers with children (51 percent). Even the British government was so concerned that it appointed its first Minister for Loneliness back in 2018.

Feelings of loneliness are subjective, of course. We all have different thresholds for the gap between the level of connection we want and the level of connection we have. But clearly we have a problem that is not getting better. So what do we do about it?

Start by asking for help from those you want to help: Okay, this sounds odd, but asking for help from those in your community—person to person—makes the giver feel more connected to you through the act of helping you. And many times, the giver of the gift feels more rewarded than the receiver. This is why when I'm running an event, I ask audience members to do some small *favor* to help out the event. Psychology research has shown that asking for a small favor from a stranger can create a deeper connection more quickly than not asking at all. Research also suggests that people with more social support tend to enjoy more positive psychological and physiological benefits. When we're able to lean on others—and support them in return—we can also be rewarded with longer, happier lives.

Restructure our life around people instead of work: I am an absolute self-proclaimed workaholic. I love what I do and want to do the best I can at it in service of others through my work. But I know that my work can't consume my entire life, that having regular connections with others is what gives me the fuel to continue my work. Having lived internationally and moved across many cities, my close circle of friends span states and countries, but technology allows me to maintain close relationships with those who feed my soul. Whenever I feel overwhelmed by the world, I make myself reach out to my circle. In turn, I will expend time, energy, and money to connect and support them back. Every time we connect, I build an even stronger foundation of positivity and trust.

Focus on high-value and low-cost interactions: High-value relationships provide deep connection and rejuvenate us, but low-cost interactions also play an important part in building courage through connection. Low-cost interactions are those we should be doing every day: saying hi to the barista, using the human checkout line instead of the computer one, smiling at your neighbors, and waving hello. These low-cost interactions feel really mundane—because they are—but studies have shown they're also a key aspect of our happiness formula, making it easier for us to connect more deeply with the high-value humans in our life. Spending time with others and connecting with them releases oxytocin and dopamine, which work together to shrink your fears and boost your bravery. By creating a feel-good cycle of bond–reward–repeat, oxytocin and dopamine help make it more likely that you'll seek out friendships and intimate connections again.

Quality over quantity: Over the years I taught environmental sustainability, I always talked about the idea of quality over quantity in how we consume products. I tried to get students to reject fast fashion that only lasts for a few washes and instead choose clothing they can wear for years and years (I have a few items I still wear from high school, which was decades ago!). In terms of building courage, quality over quantity means increasing the value you place on people and experiences. Having a lot of fast friends (those who are only friendly when it's easy and convenient and, like fast fashion, don't stand the test of time) is not the cure for loneliness—high-value relationships are.

Danger bonding: For adults, creating and maintaining such relationships is usually easier said than done. I was a digital nomad without an office long before it was cool, and making friends in a new city is not always the easiest. The obvious places for me to start were groups that did the things I liked to do or wanted to try. But here's what I found: The deepest relationships happen the quickest while doing things that are scary. Feeling, navigating, and successfully coming to the other side of fear quickly bonds humans together. I actually enjoy being scared by the more extreme side of sports—whitewater rafting, surfing, scuba diving—but if that's not your cup of tea, going to a gathering and finding the person who is hiding in the corner to befriend is another one of my tricks. No matter what the venue, most people are eager to share their stories and experiences, and when you frame the sharing as a gift they're giving you, deeper connections can flow.

Be in service to others: A 2018 study found that our amygdala is calm when we're actively engaged in service to others. It's important to note that this fear-reducing, amygdala-calming experience was not seen when those same individuals were engaged in giving to a faceless cause, only when they believed they were being generous or in service to a specific person. This can look like volunteering in your community where you're coming into contact with others, dedicating your time regularly to a group (think soccer coach or scout leader), or even just being in service of those you know, like gifting some babysitting time to a new mom or sharing a meal with an elderly neighbor.

No matter how you do it, the key to overcoming loneliness is connecting with others in courageous ways. To build meaningful connections, start by understanding the underlying fears preventing you from making connections. Loneliness is often rooted in underlying worries of being judged or rejected, so it takes a lot of moxie to push past them to build and maintain high-value connections.

When we live courageously, we all win because courage is at the heart of change.

Change Yourself; Change the World

The science of living with courage has come a long way over the past few decades, giving us access to groundbreaking research about how we can become more courageous and live with less fear every day. Don't worry, you don't have to do everything you learned in *Brave New You*. But you now have the basic tools to conquer your fears and start living with greater confidence, joy, and fulfillment.

My darkest times have been when I was so mired in my own suffering that I couldn't see beyond it. My greatest times—not the easiest, but the greatest—have been when I was able to find the courage to do something that made the world a better place. Even the process of writing this book changed me in ways I didn't see coming, pushing me to face my own fears of failure, inadequacy, and control. However, knowing that by sharing these concepts and my own struggles I had a chance of making the world a better place than I found it, even if just by a tiny bit, helped me push through the "I'm not good enough" fears of producing the manuscript. Writing this book helped me live more courageously, and I hope that reading it does the same for you.

I know it can feel hard to start, but I promise that if you take just one step forward, things will get better, even when it feels like there's no way out.

This is a lifelong process. With practice, you can move closer to a life of true bravery that will challenge you and bring you joy. Living courageously can open up possibilities you may not have imagined before and allow you to experience life more fully.

If you're like me, you'll stumble along the way, but those stumbles can also make the best stories! I know it can feel hard to start, but I promise that if you take just one step forward, things will get better, even when it feels like there's no way out. The courage to push through our fears makes us strong and allows us to reach for bigger dreams than we ever thought possible. When we embrace courage, we can lead the way toward a better future where the world is full of hope, possibility, and respect.

This is the you I see on the other side of fear: Your long-forgotten dreams are coming alive as never before, with new possibilities around every corner! Your relationships with others are deepening as trust grows stronger each day because your newfound vulnerability is building bridges instead of walls. You are seeing previously unseen beauty in everyday moments and having more profound experiences during special occasions.

May You Always Dive Deeper

Traveling solo is somewhat usual for me, but scuba diving is not a solo sport. Even though I am very much a novice diver, I somehow shamboozled a wonderful group of advanced divers to let me join their Caribbean trip off the coast of Belize's Ambergris Cay.

On the day in question, the sun was bright and the water a calm mix of emeralds and sapphires. As the forty-five minutes of our boat ride to the first dive spot began to tick away, the skies got darker and the water choppier. Fifteen minutes out, and the thrashing of our tiny dive boat had made me sicker than the morning after a Las Vegas bachelorette party. As the storm continued to ratchet up, with the winds increasing the swells every minute, we finally arrived at the dive site. Everyone geared up and back-dove in, knowing that life would be much calmer under the waves than on top.

My nausea had me moving the slowest, and I was the second-to-last diver in the water. As is customary, especially when the divemaster sees someone as inexperienced as me, they're the last one to enter the water. My seasickness, combined with the pelting rain and thrashing waves, led to my first-ever panic attack.

In every quickening, shallow breath, I gasped out, "I'm going to drown. I can't. I'm going to vomit at depth and drown. I need to get back on the boat."

Luckily, I had a very seasoned divemaster, who was having none of my foolishness.

He grabbed my BCD (buoyancy compensator device, which looks like a life jacket with extra tools), looked me dead in the eyes, and said, "Trust your training and dive deep beneath the waves. That is the best place for you to stop suffering. If you stay up here, with the rain and the waves slapping you in the face, you're just going to get sicker and sicker. If you want to feel better, trust your training and dive."

Then, he unceremoniously shoved my regulator in my mouth and deflated the air out of my BCD, descending me to the depths. No further questions asked.

Our first stop was at seventy-five feet, and the rest of the crew was already at depth, waiting for us, so I got to add embarrassment to the laundry list of the day's physical and emotional turmoil.

I was so focused on descending I almost missed the transition into another world. Sound is different that deep underwater, and the steady whooshing of sand and salt across your face is a gentle reminder that this is a place few humans see. With giant manta rays gliding below my fins, I was box breathing my butt off and finally started to at least toggle between "This is the most magical experience ever" and "Oh sweet goddess of the deep, I am going to vomit and die."

But, true to the divemaster's word, the depths were peaceful and calm even as the storm raged at the surface. It was then that I realized that the divemaster had inadvertently made this experience a metaphor for my work in navigating tough emotions like fear and courage. Given the lack of awareness, knowledge, and wisdom about how to navigate our own difficult emotions, we stay on the surface, afraid . . . often terrified to go deeper.

We think the deep is the danger.

But in fact, it's staying on the surface—where we're thrashed about, constantly pelted in the face, our energy bled away as we struggle and get sicker—that's far riskier. We will never change the storm, but we can change where we exist. Leaving the surface, diving deeper, and trusting our training will help bring us to a new world full of wonder and awe.

As our journey together comes to a close, I wish for you a long and healthy life filled with an abundance of time spent with those you love, and for you to grow and constantly learn. I know you now have the training you need to start diving deeper. To go to depths you never thought possible (even when they are scary as hell and you think you're going to vomit).

Remember, you're capable of far more than you give yourself credit for. You have already made immense strides toward living a more courageous life by trying out the neurohacks in this book. Moving forward, keep living boldly, even if it means taking small, steady steps. You have the power to choose bravery in any given moment, even when faced with difficult circumstances. As you face new fears, keep reminding yourself of your own strength and resilience.

May you always dive deeper, either by choice or with a little help, and find the awe and wonder of living with a truly courageous mind.

When you change yourself, you change the world.

Sources

CHAPTER 1

Mental Health America. "Mental Health and COVID-19 2021 Data." Accessed October 2, 2023. https://mhanational.org/mental-health-and-covid-19 -april-2022-data.

Mental Health America. "Adult Data 2022." Accessed October 2, 2023. https:// mhanational.org/issues/2022/mental-health-america-adult-data#four.

National Archives. "13th Amendment to the U.S. Constitution: Abolition of Slavery (1865)." Accessed October 2, 2023. https://www.archives.gov /milestone-documents/13th-amendment.

Psychology Today. "Default Mode Network." Accessed October 2, 2023. https:// www.psychologytoday.com/us/basics/default-mode-network.

Zheng, Weimin, Zhuangzhi Su, Xingyun Liu, Hao Zhang, Ying Han, Haiqing Song, Jie Lu, Kuncheng Li, and Zhiqun Wang. "Modulation of functional activity and connectivity by acupuncture in patients with Alzheimer disease as measured by resting-state fMRI." PloS One 13, no. 5 (2018): e0196933.

CHAPTER 2

Barajas, Joshua. "After RBG's Death, This Poet Urges Us to Follow in Her Steps." Accessed October 2, 2023. https://www.pbs.org/newshour/arts/poetry/after -rbgs-death-this-poet-urges-us-to-follow-in-her-steps.

Federal Bureau of Investigation. "Crime Data Explorer." Accessed October 2, 2023. https://cde.ucr.cjis.gov/LATEST/webapp/#/pages/home.

National Geographic. "Tardigrade." Accessed October 2, 2023." https://www .nationalgeographic.com/animals/invertebrates/facts/tardigrades-water-bears.

Nolen-Hoeksema, Susan. "The role of rumination in depressive disorders and mixed anxiety/depressive symptoms." *Journal of Abnormal Psychology* 109, no. 3 (2000): 504.

Puma. "How You Play Is What You Are: Fearless. Puma Launches the Fearless Pack." Accessed October 2, 2023. https://about.puma.com/en/newsroom /brand-and-product-news/2022/10-05-2022-fearless-pack.

ScienceDirect. "Urbach-Wiethe Disease—An Overview." Accessed October 2, 2023. https://www.sciencedirect.com/topics/biochemistry-genetics-and -molecular-biology/urbach-wiethe-disease.

Vicary, Amanda M., and R. Chris Fraley. "Captured by true crime: Why are women drawn to tales of rape, murder, and serial killers?" *Social Psychological and Personality Science* 1, no. 1 (2010): 81–86.

YouTube. "Find your Fearless | PUMA Introduces the Generation Fearless Campaign." Accessed October 2, 2023. https://www.youtube.com /watch?v=9m-WTobPA-A.

CHAPTER 3

Blacher, Suzan. "Emotional Freedom Technique (EFT): Tap to relieve stress and burnout." *Journal of Interprofessional Education & Practice* 30 (2023): 100599.

Bowlby, John. *Attachment*. Basic Books, 2008.

Byron, Kristin, Shalini Khazanchi, and Deborah Nazarian. "The relationship between stressors and creativity: A meta-analysis examining competing theoretical models." *Journal of Applied Psychology* 95, no. 1 (2010): 201.

Church, Dawson PhD, Crystal Med Hawk, Audrey J. Brooks PhD, Olli Toukolehto MD, Maria Wren LCSW, Ingrid Dinter, and Phyllis Stein PhD. "Psychological Trauma Symptom Improvement in Veterans Using Emotional Freedom Techniques: A Randomized Controlled Trial." The *Journal of Nervous and Mental Disease* 201, no. 2 (February 2013): 153–60. DOI: 10.1097 /NMD.0b013e31827f6351.

CNN. "Mandela in His Own Words." Accessed October 2, 2023. https://edition .cnn.com/2008/WORLD/africa/06/24/mandela.quotes/.

Wati, Nenden Lesmana, Tukimin Bin Sansuwito, Ramesh Prasath Rai, Irma Darmawati, Reni Anggareni, Mayasyanti Dewi Amir, and Titin Nasiatin. "The Effect of EFT (Emotional Freedom Technique) to the Self Esteem among Nurses." *Malaysian Journal of Medicine & Health Sciences* 18 (2022).

CHAPTER 4

Bathina, Siresha, and Undurti N. Das. "Brain-derived neurotrophic factor and its clinical implications." *Archives of Medical Science* 11, no. 6 (2015): 1164–78.

Forster, Gina L., Andrew M. Novick, Jamie L. Scholl, and Michael J. Watt. "The Role of the Amygdala in Anxiety Disorders." In *The Amygdala: A Discrete Multitasking Manager*, 61–102. Rijeka: InTech, 2012.

Frith, Chris, and Ray Dolan. "The role of the prefrontal cortex in higher cognitive functions." *Cognitive Brain Research* 5, no. 1–2 (1996): 175–81.

Guzmán, Yomayra F., Natalie C. Tronson, Vladimir Jovasevic, Keisuke Sato, Anita L. Guedea, Hiroaki Mizukami, Katsuhiko Nishimori, and Jelena Radulovic. "Fear-enhancing effects of septal oxytocin receptors." *Nature Neuroscience* 16, no. 9 (2013): 1185–87.

Lin, Shih-Hsien, Lan-Ting Lee, and Yen Kuang Yang. "Serotonin and mental disorders: A concise review on molecular neuroimaging evidence." *Clinical Psychopharmacology and Neuroscience* 12, no. 3 (2014): 196.

McCarty, R. "The Fight-or-Flight Response: A Cornerstone of Stress Research." In *Stress: Concepts, Cognition, Emotion, and Behavior*, 33–37. Academic Press, 2016.

Monfils, Marie-H. "Revisiting MacLean: The Limbic System and Emotional Behavior," 103. In *Brain and Behaviour: Revisiting the Classic Studies*. SAGE Publications, 2017.

Mushiake, Hajime, Kazuhiro Sakamoto, Naohiro Saito, Toshiro Inui, Kazuyuki Aihara, and Jun Tanji. "Involvement of the prefrontal cortex in problem solving." *International Review of Neurobiology* 85 (2009): 1–11.

Nili, Uri, Hagar Goldberg, Abraham Weizman, and Yadin Dudai. "Fear thou not: Activity of frontal and temporal circuits in moments of real-life courage." *Neuron* 66, no. 6 (2010): 949–62.

Paul, Ian A., and Phil Skolnick. "Glutamate and depression: clinical and preclinical studies." *Annals of the New York Academy of Sciences* 1003, no. 1 (2003): 250–72.

Rajmohan, V., and E. Mohandas. "The limbic system." *Indian Journal of Psychiatry* 49, no. 2 (2007): 132.

Ressler, Kerry J. "Amygdala activity, fear, and anxiety: modulation by stress." *Biological Psychiatry* 67, no. 12 (2010): 1117–19.

Taylor, Warren D., David H. Zald, Jennifer C. Felger, Seth Christman, Daniel O. Claassen, Guillermo Horga, Jeffrey M. Miller, et al. "Influences of dopaminergic system dysfunction on late-life depression." *Molecular Psychiatry* 27, no. 1 (2022): 180–91.

CHAPTER 5

Byron, Kristin, Shalini Khazanchi, and Deborah Nazarian. "The relationship between stressors and creativity: A meta-analysis examining competing theoretical models." *Journal of Applied Psychology* 95, no. 1 (2010): 201.

Gump, Brooks B., and James A. Kulik. "Stress, affiliation, and emotional contagion." *Journal of Personality and Social Psychology* 72, no. 2 (1997): 305.

Kanske, Philipp, and Sonja A. Kotz. "Emotion triggers executive attention: Anterior cingulate cortex and amygdala responses to emotional words in a conflict task." *Human Brain Mapping* 32, no. 2 (2011): 198–208.

Kilner, James M., and Roger N. Lemon. "What we know currently about mirror neurons." *Current Biology* 23, no. 23 (2013): R1057–62.

Ray, William J., Christine Molnar, Deane Aikins, Alissa Yamasaki, Michelle G. Newman, Louis Castonguay, and Thomas D. Borkovec. "Startle response in generalized anxiety disorder." *Depression and Anxiety* 26, no. 2 (2009): 147–54.

Pendell, Ryan. "Customer Brand Preference and Decisions: Gallup's 70/30 Principle." Accessed October 2, 2023. https://www.gallup.com/workplace/398954/customer-brand-preference-decisions-gallup-principle.aspx.

CHAPTER 6

Blades, Robin. "Protecting the brain against bad news." *Canadian Medical Association Journal* 193, no. 12 (March 2021): E428–29.

Byyny, Richard L. "Information and cognitive overload." *Pharos* 79, no. 4 (Autumn 2016).

Farías, Pablo. "The use of fear versus hope in health advertisements: The moderating role of individual characteristics on subsequent health decisions in Chile." *International Journal of Environmental Research and Public Health* 17, no. 23 (2020): 9148.

Festinger, Leon. "A theory of social comparison processes." *Human Relations* 7, no. 2 (1954): 117–40.

Holman, E. Alison, Dana Rose Garfin, and Roxane Cohen Silver. "Media's role in broadcasting acute stress following the Boston Marathon bombings." *Proceedings of the National Academy of Sciences* 111, no. 1 (2014): 93–98.

Milkman, Katherine, Liz Rees-Jones, and Jonah Berger. "The secret to online success: What makes content go viral." *Scientific American* (April 14, 2015).

Ozbay, Fatih, Douglas C. Johnson, Eleni Dimoulas, C. A. Morgan Iii, Dennis Charney, and Steven Southwick. "Social support and resilience to stress: From neurobiology to clinical practice." *Psychiatry (Edgmont)* 4, no. 5 (2007): 35.

Pollock, Samara, Susan Taylor, Oyetewa Oyerinde, Sabrina Nurmohamed, Ncoza Dlova, Rashmi Sarkar, Hassan Galadari, et al. "The dark side of skin lightening: An international collaboration and review of a public health issue affecting dermatology." *International Journal of Women's Dermatology* 7, no. 2 (2021): 158–64.

Reedy, Katherine. "Ads pressure Hong Kong women to whiten up." *Women's E News* (2009).

Vijaya, Ramya M. "Dangerous skin bleaching has become a public health crisis. Corporate marketing lies behind it." *Washington Post*, June 15, 2019.

Voultsos, Polychronis, Maria Koungali, Konstantinos Psaroulis, and Afroditi K. Boutou. "Burnout syndrome and its association with anxiety and fear of medical errors among intensive care unit physicians: A cross-sectional study." *Anaesthesia and Intensive Care* 48, no. 2 (2020): 134–42.

CHAPTER 7

Bögels, Susan M., and Warren Mansell. "Attention processes in the maintenance and treatment of social phobia: Hypervigilance, avoidance and self-focused attention." *Clinical Psychology Review* 24, no. 7 (2004): 827–56.

Butterhof, Jannis. "Understanding the Mindtrap: How Irrational Thinking Affects Risk-Anticipation in Work-Related Decision-Making. A Correlative Study." Thesis, July 2016.

Cox, Rebecca D. "Promoting Success by Addressing Students' Fear of Failure." *Community College Review* 37, no. 1 (2009).

de Lima, Miguel Antonio Xavier, Marcus Vinicius C. Baldo, Fernando A. Oliveira, and Newton Sabino Canteras. "The anterior cingulate cortex and its role in controlling contextual fear memory to predatory threats." *ELife* 11 (2022): e67007.

Kahneman, Daniel. *Thinking, Fast and Slow*. Macmillan, 2011, 23

Kleshchova, Olena, Jenna K. Rieder, Jack Grinband, and Mariann R. Weierich. "Resting amygdala connectivity and basal sympathetic tone as markers of chronic hypervigilance." *Psychoneuroendocrinology* 102 (2019): 68–78.

Lipsky, Rachele K., Catherine C. McDonald, Margaret C. Souders, Claudia C. Carpio, and Anne M. Teitelman. "Adverse childhood experiences, the serotonergic system, and depressive and anxiety disorders in adulthood: A systematic literature review." *Neuroscience & Biobehavioral Reviews* 134 (2022): 104495.

Luberto, C., S. Cotton, and A. McLeish. "OA14.01. Relaxation-induced anxiety: Predictors and subjective explanations among young adults." *BMC Complementary and Alternative Medicine* 12 (2012): 1-1.

Rolls, Edmund T. "The cingulate cortex and limbic systems for emotion, action, and memory." *Brain Structure and Function* 224, no. 9 (2019): 3001–18.

Sakulku, Jaruwan. "The impostor phenomenon." *Journal of Behavioral Science* 6, no. 1 (2011): 75–97.

Schlund, Michael W., and Michael F. Cataldo. "Amygdala involvement in human avoidance, escape and approach behavior." *Neuroimage* 53, no. 2 (2010): 769–76.

Steenland, Hendrik W., Xiang-Yao Li, and Min Zhuo. "Predicting aversive events and terminating fear in the mouse anterior cingulate cortex during trace fear conditioning." *Journal of Neuroscience* 32, no. 3 (2012): 1082–95.

CHAPTER 8

Abraham, Wickliffe C., Owen D. Jones, and David L. Glanzman. "Is plasticity of synapses the mechanism of long-term memory storage?" *NPJ Science of Learning* 4, no. 1 (2019): 9.

American Psychological Association. "Stress Effects on the Body." Accessed October 2, 2023. https://www.apa.org/topics/stress/body.

Hamasaki, Hidetaka. "Effects of diaphragmatic breathing on health: A narrative review." *Medicines* 7, no. 10 (2020): 65.

Masuo, Yoshinori, Tadaaki Satou, Hiroaki Takemoto, and Kazuo Koike. "Smell and stress response in the brain: Review of the connection between chemistry and neuropharmacology." *Molecules* 26, no. 9 (2021): 2571.

Plutchik, Robert. "The nature of emotions: Human emotions have deep evolutionary roots, a fact that may explain their complexity and provide tools for clinical practice." *American Scientist* 89, no. 4 (2001): 344–350.

Sagi, Yaniv, Ido Tavor, Shir Hofstetter, Shimrit Tzur-Moryosef, Tamar Blumenfeld-Katzir, and Yaniv Assaf. "Learning in the fast lane: New insights into neuroplasticity." *Neuron* 73, no. 6 (2012): 1195–1203.

Strimbu, Kyle, and Jorge A. Tavel. "What are biomarkers?" *Current Opinion in HIV and AIDS* 5, no. 6 (2010): 463.

Ullrich, Philip M., and Susan K. Lutgendorf. "Journaling about stressful events: Effects of cognitive processing and emotional expression." *Annals of Behavioral Medicine* 24, no. 3 (2002): 244–50.

Wexler, Anna. "The social context of 'do-it-yourself' brain stimulation: Neurohackers, biohackers, and lifehackers." *Frontiers in Human Neuroscience* 11 (2017): 224.

CHAPTER 9

Barrett, Frederick S., Kevin J. Grimm, Richard W. Robins, Tim Wildschut, Constantine Sedikides, and Petr Janata. "Music-evoked nostalgia: Affect, memory, and personality." *Emotion* 10, no. 3 (2010): 390.

Ben-Menachem, E., A. Hamberger, T. Hedner, E. J. Hammond, B. M. Uthman, J. Slater, T. Treig, et al. "Effects of vagus nerve stimulation on amino acids and other metabolites in the CSF of patients with partial seizures." *Epilepsy Research* 20, no. 3 (1995): 221–27.

Datta, Avijit, and Michael Tipton. "Respiratory responses to cold water immersion: Neural pathways, interactions, and clinical consequences awake and asleep." *Journal of Applied Physiology* 100, no. 6 (2006): 2057–64.

Eid, Charlotte M., Colin Hamilton, and Joanna MH Greer. "Untangling the tingle: Investigating the association between the Autonomous Sensory Meridian Response (ASMR), neuroticism, and trait & state anxiety." Plos One 17, no. 2 (2022): e0262668.

Ellingsen, Dan-Mikael, Siri Leknes, Guro Løseth, Johan Wessberg, and Håkan Olausson. "The neurobiology shaping affective touch: Expectation, motivation, and meaning in the multisensory context." *Frontiers in Psychology* 6 (2016): 1986.

Feinstein, Justin S., Sahib S. Khalsa, Hung Yeh, Obada Al Zoubi, Armen C. Arevian, Colleen Wohlrab, Marie K. Pantino, et al. "The elicitation of relaxation and interoceptive awareness using floatation therapy in individuals with high anxiety sensitivity." *Biological Psychiatry: Cognitive Neuroscience and Neuroimaging* 3, no. 6 (2018): 555–62.

George, Mark S., Herbert E. Ward Jr., Philip T. Ninan, Mark Pollack, Ziad Nahas, Berry Anderson, Samet Kose, Robert H. Howland, Wayne K. Goodman, and James C. Ballenger. "A pilot study of vagus nerve stimulation (VNS) for treatment-resistant anxiety disorders." *Brain Stimulation* 1, no. 2 (2008): 112–21.

Hamasaki, Hidetaka. "Effects of diaphragmatic breathing on health: A narrative review." *Medicines* 7, no. 10 (2020): 65.

Holland, Taylor Mallory. "Facts About Touch: How Human Contact Affects Your Health and Relationships." https://www.dignityhealth.org/articles/facts-about-touch-how-human-contact-affects-your-health-and-relationships.

Hopper, Susan I., Sherrie L. Murray, Lucille R. Ferrara, and Joanne K. Singleton. "Effectiveness of diaphragmatic breathing for reducing physiological and psychological stress in adults: A quantitative systematic review." *JBI Evidence Synthesis* 17, no. 9 (2019): 1855–76.

Isik, B. K., A. Esen, B. Büyükerkmen, A. Kilinc, and D. J. B. J. Menziletoglu. "Effectiveness of binaural beats in reducing preoperative dental anxiety." *British Journal of Oral and Maxillofacial Surgery* 55, no. 6 (2017): 571–74.

Jansen, Arthur SP, Xay Van Nguyen, Vladimir Karpitskiy, Thomas C. Mettenleiter, and Arthur D. Loewy. "Central command neurons of the sympathetic nervous system: Basis of the fight-or-flight response." *Science* 270, no. 5236 (1995): 644–46.

Kapp, Steven K., Robyn Steward, Laura Crane, Daisy Elliott, Chris Elphick, Elizabeth Pellicano, and Ginny Russell. "'People should be allowed to do what they like': Autistic adults' views and experiences of stimming." *Autism* 23, no. 7 (2019): 1782–92.

Lesiuk, Teresa. "The effect of preferred music on mood and performance in a high-cognitive demand occupation." *Journal of Music Therapy* 47, no. 2 (2010): 137–54.

Meier, Maria, Eva Unternaehrer, Stephanie J. Dimitroff, Annika BE Benz, Ulrike U. Bentele, Sabine M. Schorpp, Maya Wenzel, and Jens C. Pruessner. "Standardized massage interventions as protocols for the induction of psychophysiological relaxation in the laboratory: A block randomized, controlled trial." Scientific Reports 10, no. 1 (2020): 14774.

Mönnikes, H., J. J. Tebbe, M. Hildebrandt, P. Arck, E. Osmanoglou, M. Rose, B. Klapp, B. Wiedenmann, and I. Heymann-Mönnikes. "Role of stress in functional gastrointestinal disorders: Evidence for stress-induced alterations in gastrointestinal motility and sensitivity." *Digestive Diseases* 19, no. 3 (2001): 201–11.

Munawar, Khadeeja, Sara K. Kuhn, and Shamsul Haque. "Understanding the reminiscence bump: A systematic review." PloS One 13, no. 12 (2018): e0208595.

Padmanabhan, R., A. J. Hildreth, and D. Laws. "A prospective, randomised, controlled study examining binaural beat audio and pre?operative anxiety in patients undergoing general anaesthesia for day case surgery." *Anaesthesia* 60, no. 9 (2005): 874–77.

Panchal, Saharsh, Fariburz Irani, and Gunjan Y. Trivedi. "Impact of Himalayan singing bowls meditation session on mood and heart rate variability." *International Journal of Psychotherapy Practice and Research* 1, no. 4 (2020): 20–29.

Wiwatwongwana, D., P. Vichitvejpaisal, L. Thaikruea, J. Klaphajone, A. Tantong, and A. Wiwatwongwana. "The effect of music with and without binaural beat audio on operative anxiety in patients undergoing cataract surgery: A randomized controlled trial." *Eye* 30, no. 11 (2016): 1407–14.

Woodard, Cooper R. "Hardiness and the concept of courage." *Consulting Psychology Journal: Practice and Research* 56, no. 3 (2004): 173.

Zaccaro, Andrea, Andrea Piarulli, Marco Laurino, Erika Garbella, Danilo Menicucci, Bruno Neri, and Angelo Gemignani. "How breath-control can change your life: A systematic review on psycho-physiological correlates of slow breathing." *Frontiers in Human Neuroscience* (2018): 353.

CHAPTER 10

Boggiss, Anna L., Nathan S. Consedine, Jennifer M. Brenton-Peters, Paul L. Hofman, and Anna S. Serlachius. "A systematic review of gratitude interventions: Effects on physical health and health behaviors." *Journal of Psychosomatic Research* 135 (2020): 110165.

Burton, Linda Roszak, BS, ACC. "The neuroscience and positive impact of gratitude in the workplace." *Journal of Medical Practice Management: MPM* 35, no. 4 (2020): 215–18.

Csikszentmihalyi, Mihaly. *Creativity: Flow and the Psychology of Discovery and Invention*. (New York: HarperPerennial, 1997), 1–16.

Collins, KC. "Pygmalion Effect," in *Encyclopedia of Child Behavior and Development*, ed. Sam Goldstein and Jack A. Naglieri. Boston: Springer, 2011.

Datu, Jesus Alfonso D., Jana Patricia M. Valdez, Dennis M. McInerney, and Ryan Francis Cayubit. "The effects of gratitude and kindness on life satisfaction, positive emotions, negative emotions, and COVID?19 anxiety: An online pilot experimental study." *Applied Psychology: Health and Well?Being* 14, no. 2 (2022): 347–61.

Encyclopedia Britannica. "Grimm's Fairy Tales." Accessed October 2, 2023. https://www.britannica.com/topic/Grimms-Fairy-Tales.

Farrow, Marc R., and Kyle Washburn. "A review of field experiments on the effect of forest bathing on anxiety and heart rate variability." *Global Advances in Health and Medicine* 8 (2019): 2164956119848654.

Fagundo, Ana Beatriz, Esther Via, Isabel Sánchez, Susana Jiménez-Murcia, Laura Forcano, Carles Soriano-Mas, Cristina Giner-Bartolomé, et al. "Physiological and brain activity after a combined cognitive behavioral treatment plus video game therapy for emotional regulation in bulimia nervosa: A case report." *Journal of Medical Internet Research* 16, no. 8 (2014): e3243.

Frankland, Paul W., Bruno Bontempi, Lynn E. Talton, Leszek Kaczmarek, and Alcino J. Silva. "The involvement of the anterior cingulate cortex in remote contextual fear memory." *Science* 304, no. 5672 (2004): 881–83.

Gluck, Kevin A., and Jayde M. King. "Cognitive Architectures for Human Factors in Aviation and Aerospace." In *Human Factors in Aviation and Aerospace*, 279–307. Academic Press, 2023.

Greipl, Simon, Elise Klein, Antero Lindstedt, Kristian Kiili, Korbinian Moeller, H. O. Karnath, Julia Bahnmueller, Johannes Bloechle, and Manuel Ninaus. "When the brain comes into play: Neurofunctional correlates of emotions and reward in game-based learning." *Computers in Human Behavior* 125 (2021): 106946.

Johnson, Daniel, Sebastian Deterding, Kerri-Ann Kuhn, Aleksandra Staneva, Stoyan Stoyanov, and Leanne Hides. "Gamification for health and wellbeing: A systematic review of the literature." *Internet Interventions* 6 (2016): 89–106.

Karns, Christina M., William E. Moore III, and Ulrich Mayr. "The cultivation of pure altruism via gratitude: A functional MRI study of change with gratitude practice." *Frontiers in Human Neuroscience* 11 (2017): 599.

Lee, Ju-Yeon, Seon-Young Kim, Kyung-Yeol Bae, Jae-Min Kim, Il-Seon Shin, Jin-Sang Yoon, and Sung-Wan Kim. "The association of gratitude with perceived stress and burnout among male firefighters in Korea." *Personality and Individual Differences* 123 (2018): 205–08.

Lu, Hsi-Peng, and Hui-Chen Ho. "Exploring the impact of gamification on users' engagement for sustainable development: A case study in brand applications." *Sustainability* 12, no. 10 (2020): 4169.

Mennin, Douglas S., Kristen K. Ellard, David M. Fresco, and James J. Gross. "United we stand: Emphasizing commonalities across cognitive-behavioral therapies." *Behavior Therapy* 44, no. 2 (2013): 234–48.

Nakamura, Jeanne, and Mihaly Csikszentmihalyi. "The concept of flow." *Handbook of Positive Psychology* 89 (2002): 105.

Nabar, M. J. M. Y., Rubén D. Algieri, and Elba B. Tornese. "Gamification or gaming techniques applied to pedagogy: Foundations of the cognitive neuroscience applied to the education." *Global Journal of Human-Social Science: Linguistics and Education* 18 (2018): 9–13.

Semkovska, Maria. "Electroconvulsive Therapy for Depression: Effectiveness, Cognitive Side-Effects, and Mechanisms of Action." In *The Neuroscience of Depression*, 527–36. Academic Press, 2021.

Stevens, Francis L., Robin A. Hurley, and Katherine H. Taber. "Anterior cingulate cortex: Unique role in cognition and emotion." *Journal of Neuropsychiatry and Clinical Neurosciences* 23, no. 2 (2011): 121–25.

Van Den Berg, Agnes E., and Mariëtte HG Custers. "Gardening promotes neuroendocrine and affective restoration from stress." *Journal of Health Psychology* 16, no. 1 (2011): 3–11.

West, G. L., K. Konishi, M. Diarra, J. Benady-Chorney, B. L. Drisdelle, L. Dahmani, D. J. Sodums, F. Lepore, P. Jolicoeur, and V. D. Bohbot. "Impact of video games on plasticity of the hippocampus." *Molecular Psychiatry* 23, no. 7 (2018): 1566–74.

Wong, Y. Joel, Jesse Owen, Nicole T. Gabana, Joshua W. Brown, Sydney McInnis, Paul Toth, and Lynn Gilman. "Does gratitude writing improve the mental health of psychotherapy clients? Evidence from a randomized controlled trial." *Psychotherapy Research* 28, no. 2 (2018): 192–202.

CHAPTER 11

Breuning, Loretta Graziano. *Habits of a Happy Brain: Retrain Your Brain to Boost Your Serotonin, Dopamine, Oxytocin, and Endorphin Levels*. Simon and Schuster, 2015.

Brown, A., Huiyi Guo, and Hyundam Je. "Preferences for the Resolution of Risk and Ambiguity." Available at SSRN 4092231 (2022).

Cacioppo, John T., and William Patrick. *Loneliness: Human Nature and the Need for Social Connection*. W.W. Norton & Company, 2008.

Choksi, Dave. "Op-Ed: NYC Health Commissioner Dr. Chokshi Says Covid Pandemic Has Left U.S. with New Epidemic of Loneliness." Accessed October 2, 2023. https://www.cnbc.com/2022/03/09/op-ed-nyc-health-commissioner-chokshi-says-covid-pandemic-has-left-us-with-new-epidemic-of-loneliness.html.

Grange Isaacson, Tyia. "Metaphors of agony: Culture-bound syndromes of hyper-independence." *Psychoanalysis, Self and Context* 15, no. 4 (2020): 375–83.

Harvard Graduate School of Education. "Loneliness in America: How the Pandemic Has Deepened an Epidemic of Loneliness and What We Can Do About It." Accessed October 2, 2023. https://mcc.gse.harvard.edu/reports/loneliness-in-america.

Harvard Medical School. "The Power of Self-Compassion." Accessed October 2, 2023. https://www.health.harvard.edu/healthbeat/the-power-of-self -compassion#:~:text=Self%2Dcompassion%20yields%20a%20number,their %20anxiety%20and%20related%20depression.

Inagaki, Tristen K., and Lauren P. Ross. "Neural correlates of giving social support: Differences between giving targeted versus untargeted support." *Psychosomatic Medicine* 80, no. 8 (2018): 724–32.

Murthy, Vivek H. "Together: The Healing Power of Human Connection in a Sometimes Lonely World." Accessed October 2, 2023. https://www. vivekmurthy.com/together-book.

The Cultural Context. "The Cultural Context." Accessed October 2, 2023. https:// www.sagepub.com/sites/default/files/upm-binaries/42958_2_The_Cultural_ Context.pdf.

Index

interactions, high- and low-value, 218
internet, and doom scrolling, 102–103

J

Jacobson, Lenore, 200
jardiner practice, 189–190
journaling, 144, 199, 207
journalism, fear-driven, 97–100
judgment, fear of, 8, 116
Junky (Burroughs), 33

K

Kahneman, Daniel, 112
Kingdom of the Feared (Maniscalco), 212
Kuhn, Maggie, 209

L

Lamott, Annie, 205
language of fear, 91–93
limbic system, 62–65
logic, versus emotions, 87–89
loneliness, 8, 31, 217–219
loss, fear of, 30
low-value interactions, 218

M

MacEwe (suprameatal) triangle, 169
Mandela, Nelson, 35
Maniscalco, Kerri, 212
marketing, fear-based, 93–95
Marvel characters, 88, 89
Matrix (film), 160
Matson, John, 85–86
McCool, William, 184
media, fear in, 97–100
mind chatter, 125
mind traps, 107, 108–109, 110–111
mirror neurons, 89–90
missing out, fear of (FOMO), 94
mistakes, fear of, 30–31
Mokhonoana, Mokokoma, 57
moral courage, 40–41
The Mortal Word (Cogman), 134
"Move Fast and Break Things," 42
murder mysteries, 27–28, 31–32
Murthy, Vivek, 217
musical playlists, 180–181
myth of fearlessness, 19–23

N

Nakamura, Jeanne, 196
naming fear, 136–137
NASA Space Shuttle *Columbia*, 184–185

Acknowledgments

Let's be real. Writing these, above almost anything else in this book, made me nervous . . . scared . . . angsty . . . because I wanted it to be perfect for all the people in my life who have sacrificed to support me, my dreams, and this book. But perfectionism is poison to progress, so here we go.

First, this book would have never seen the light of day had Aevitas agent Chelsey Heller not emailed me with the magic words, "Hey, have you thought about writing a book?" after listening to me on Alie Ward's podcast *Ologies* (thank you Alie!).

Yes is truly a magical word that ripples out to change the world.

Chelsey said yes to opportunities outside of New York City, which blossomed into the chance for me to have industry legend Toby Mundy as my agent. Toby, you took a chance on a new to trade market science nerd author, and I hope this work makes you proud. At our first meeting, I knew I wanted my book to sit on your top favourites bookshelf, and I can't wait for this cover to have its own shiny space. Thank you for your unwavering dedication and belief in me and this project.

Toby's yes resulted in a field of possibilities opening up, including meeting top Senior Editor John Meils. From the first minutes of our meeting, I knew I had to work with John and his team—and as I finish the writing of this book, I couldn't be happier with that particular yes.

John, thank you for your tireless dedication to excellence on this project and for believing in me as a creator. For showing me the ropes of publishing with the "Big Five" publishers and making this book, and me as a writer, better than I ever thought it could be.

To my ninja rockstar entertainment counsel Michele Martell of Martell Media House—I know you would fight dragons for me and win! You make me feel safe and empowered and are an inspiration to me in every arena you step into.

To my in-the-trenches editorial support team of Jessica Sindler with Kevin Anderson & Associates, Michelle Moore, and Charlene Ruell with Panache Consulting. The birthing of this book would not have been possible without your line-by-line, word-by-word support. Writing can be a lonely business, but you ensured that wasn't the case for me, which absolutely made this book—and me as a writer— so much better than it could ever have been if I tried to do it alone.

To Suzanne and Elton Selph, my safe port in any storm, my bonus parents who helped raise me. You gave me a childhood steeped in love and acceptance. You showed me how to give back to one's community and how to live with truth and honesty. Your love and guidance helped make me who I am today.

To Craig Allen, well, I wrote about you a bunch in this book, so suffice to say you must be a pretty important guy. But sass aside, you have changed my life in so many ways—with your love of adventure, with your wisdom, with your patience and kindness, and, of course, with your love. May our words, our memories, and most of all our stories long outlast our mortal shells.

To Deliah Rae Taylor—thank you for your inspirational badas- sery and for giving me a ticket to the world. Without you, being at the table or in the room would have been impossible.

To my sisters of the written word who shared their craft and their hearts with me during this journey of creation: Iris Polit, Kristin Procko, Lainey Cameron, Laura Brekke Wagoner, and L. Stephanie Tait. Your love, support, wisdom, and guidance made this book possible.

To my London SciComm family: Emma Parkin, Catherine Webb, Frances McStea, Joy Aston, Kate Smith, Keyne Rowe, and Lucy Timms-Davis. Y'all were there at the birth of this work, and through too many creative sessions to count. You have all contributed in a thousand different ways to help me become the science communicator I am today. Within our circle, I felt seen and loved. It felt like coming home. So, thank you all for being as weird as me!

To the Moore Pack, Steve, Michelle, Charlie, and Maddie, for making beach days the best days and for making me and Bandit family. Y'all are a constant inspiration for what it means to be loving and supportive and were an absolute motivator to keep moving forward.

To friends that became family, you make me a better writer by helping me live an uncommon life. One of story and adventure. One of love and laughter . . . and of wine. So much wine! Each of you has influenced me and the stories I tell in too many ways to count and listened to me drone on and on about my work. I am so grateful for you: Brielan Smiechowski, Dub Wainwright, Jenny Sonawala, Melissa Ke, Riely Allen, and Sabrina Yam.

To my fur baby, Bandit. You can't read this, but this book wouldn't have been possible without the stalwart companionship, unwavering devotion, and never-ending comfort you provided for the low, low price of high-end fancy treats.

Last but not least, this book wouldn't have happened without Momma Helen. Complicated and problematic, but I know she did the best she could with the tools she had. In her own way, she loved fiercely. As we all try to do.

Every one of you has given me a key to open a new door, irrevocably changing my life forever.

For that, and for you, I will be forever grateful. I love you all.